No Downtime

No Downtime

SIX STEPS TO INDUSTRIAL PROBLEM SOLVING

L. E. Cook, Jr.

Addison-Wesley Publishing Company, Inc.

Reading, Massachusetts • Menlo Park, California • New York
Don Mills, Ontario • Wokingham, England • Amsterdam • Bonn • Sydney
Singapore • Tokyo • Madrid • San Juan

Many of the designations used by manufacturers and sellers to distinguish their products are claimed as trademarks. Where those designations appear in this book and Addison-Wesley was aware of a trademark claim, the designations have been printed in initial caps.

Library of Congress Cataloging-in-Publication Data

Cook, L. E.
No downtime / L. E. Cook, Jr.
p. cm.
ISBN 0-201-55065-2 (acid-free paper)
1. Production management. I. Title.
TS155.C6375 1991
658.5—dc20 90-38347
CIP

The publisher offers discounts on this book when ordered in quantity for special sales. For more information please contact:

Corporate & Professional Publishing Group
Addison-Wesley Publishing Company
Route 128
Reading, Massachusetts 01867

Sponsoring Editor, Ted Buswick
Cover design by Absolute Design Services
Text design by Wilson Graphics and Design (Kenneth J. Wilson)
Set in 10 point Bookman by Compset

ISBN 0-201-55065-2

Printed on recycled and acid-free paper

ABCDEFGHIJ-BK-9543210
First Printing, November 1990

Contents

Chapter 1

WHY WE NEED A FORMAL PROCESS

As organizational cultures begin to change, organizational members will be invited to participate in the solving of everyday business problems.

Typically, we tend to use the old "Who?" style of thinking:

Thinking Process (Old Style)

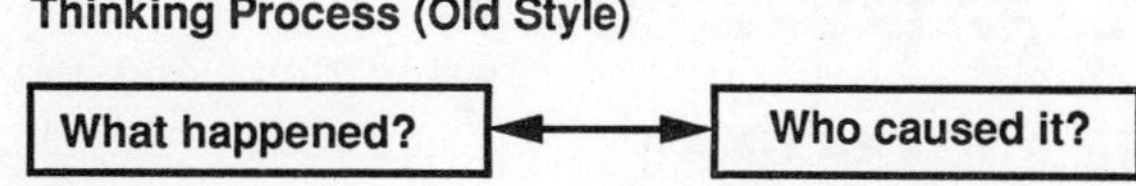

This is ineffective at best and alienates those involved. The only effective approach to problem solving is the "cause-and-effect" style of thinking:

Thinking Process (New Style)

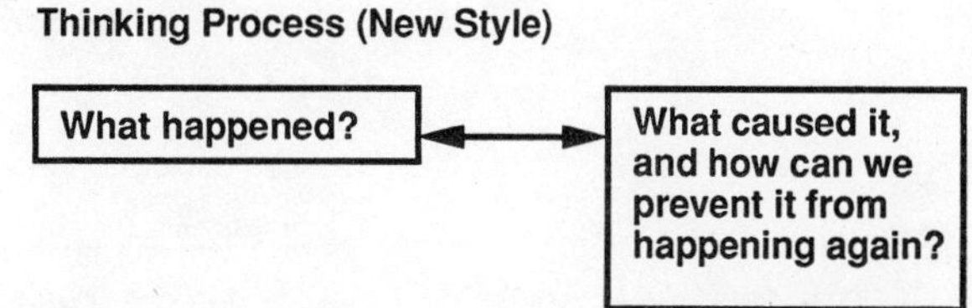

To facilitate this change in thinking style, I have developed a formal process for solving problems. One of the first questions you might ask is, "Why do I need training in problem solving when I already know how to solve problems?"

Just remember, problem solving is a skill, and like any skill, it can be learned. Once learned, it may be continually improved upon. Some people have a natural ability for solving problems, but even they can improve upon and polish their skills.

Problem-solving skills and an organizational attitude that allows problems to surface rather than covering problems over are both essential to a philosophy of continuous improvement and ultimate customer satisfaction.

As an employee, it is important that you be able to solve problems and that you approach problem solving with an alert mind and a positive attitude. A training program in problem solving will improve your skills and help you see that it really is necessary and possible to solve the problems you see around you in the workplace.

It also helps develop a common language that everyone knows and can understand.

One way of developing the skills you need to solve problems is to learn a formal process for doing so and to follow it like a road map. The formal process I present here includes some of the tools and techniques you will need to move through it, either as an individual or as a member of a team or group, in a step-by-step manner until you reach your goal.

This process is, in fact, a scientific method of problem solving, grounded in reality and based on solid facts. It will require you to collect and deal with information in one or more of the following ways.

COLLECTING AND ACCESSING INFORMATION

OBSERVE AND DOCUMENT JOB ELEMENTS

In order to really understand what you are doing, it may be necessary for you to observe and document the elements of the actual work you are required to do to complete the job. You can do this by sitting down and listing everything you do during the day or during a normal work cycle. At this time, the order is not important; the idea is to get a complete list. Recording job elements helps because it allows you to look at the content of the job or work routine objectively.

Example:

Your job is to assemble a heat shield to a much larger component as it passes by your workstation. To accomplish this you are required to do the following six tasks:

Task #	*Description*
1	Take shield from box.
2	Take 2 bolts from stock tray on right.
3	Take 2 lock washers from stock tray on left.
4	Subassemble the bolts to the shield.
5	Using the air tool provided, attach heat shield subassembly to the main assembly.
6	Check the torque on both the sub- and main assemblies every 25 cycles.

IDENTIFY AND ANALYZE THE CURRENT METHOD

Once you have documented the current job elements, it helps to put them in the sequence in which they are performed. This is the first step in identifying and analyzing your daily work routine. Using the job elements (tasks) listed in the example above, you will analyze your current method of processing the product. Begin by asking yourself:

- Is the sequence of events correct?
- Am I using the right tools?

- Is the frequency I torque check correct?
- Etc.

IDENTIFY THE POSSIBLE CONTRIBUTING CAUSES

At this point you will begin to look for possible causes of the current problem, or in the case of an area needing continuous improvement, this is where you look for inefficient methods. Open-mindedness is of key importance at this stage as you begin to compare the process and the problem looking for possible causes. One way of doing this is called brainstorming, which is described in Chapter 3. Another is to develop some kind of cause-and-effect diagram. A simple cause-and-effect diagram—using our example—might look like this:

Cause	Effect
Air pressure is low>>>>>>>>	<<<Improper torque
Torque wrench not calibrated>>	<<<Improper torque
Wrong bolts in stock tray >>>>	<<<Unable to assemble

DEVELOPING NEW IDEAS

It is here that you begin to formulate the ideas necessary to correct the problem you have identified. Write down as many solutions as you can think of. Then, through a structured process of evaluation, select the most logical solution. These techniques are described later in the book.

IMPLEMENTATION, EVALUATION, AND SHARING

This is the stage where you or your group put together everything you have done up to this point. The problem has been identified and analyzed and the solution has been decided upon. It is now time to figure out how to implement it. At this step, you will be developing time lines and deciding what types of resources you need to put your ideas to work. The resources are lined up, the materials required are on hand, and the operation or process is available.

Once the improvement has been implemented, it is not necessarily time to stop. At this point all the information necessary to prove (or disprove) the impact the change really made must be collected. Only by evaluating the results can it be determined if the implemented change had any real effect.

The improvement may have value in other places in your organization. To ensure that your idea gets proper exposure, you may want to prepare a presentation for the group, or turn in a suggestion.

A note about suggestions and suggestion programs. To me, there are two types of suggestion programs, passive and active. In the passive system, employees turn in written suggestions only to have them sit around on someone's desk. Or worse yet, a suggestion is returned to the employee with a letter stating flatly that the idea has no value, with no personal feedback. In an active suggestion program solutions and implementation are considered to be one continuous effort and employees are encouraged to participate through feedback and through the implementation process.

CONSTRUCTIVE SUGGESTIONS VERSUS COMPLAINTS

When there is dissatisfaction with some thing or situation, progress can only be made when there is also a willingness to correct it. Complaining is being dissatisfied with the current situation but unwilling to work at correcting it. Complaints hinder progress. They create low morale and cause the atmosphere of the workplace to deteriorate. In fact, they are the first step backward. Complaints, unless they include constructive suggestions or positive alternatives for improvement, never solve problems.

If you are dissatisfied with the existing situation, it is essential that you or your group promote the ideas necessary to improve it. The best person to come up with the most constructive ideas will be the person who is most familiar with the job, the one who does it every day.

BECOMING AWARE OF PROBLEMS

Everyone must be aware of the problems that are faced in the workplace. Be clear about which ones require immediate attention and why. Decide, as an individual or as a group, the problem you will begin with. The greater the number of problems, the more important it becomes to have a system for prioritizing them. To gain experience, start with a small yet persistent problem. Solving it will give you the confidence and courage you need to move on to bigger problems.

Too often we are content to see people work and machines operate without any major disasters. But such appearances do not necessarily mean that the job is running smoothly, nor that you may relax. You will never detect problems as long as you look at the current situation casually.

Problem resolution or continuous improvement cannot be carried out with a mind-set that says, "There are no particular problems in the current way we are doing it," or if the current method is accepted as the "best way." In order for organizations to keep pace in today's marketplace, they must continually look for ways to improve their products and the processes that produce them. In other words, "good enough" isn't good enough anymore.

To discover areas where a formal problem-solving process can be applied, all you have to do is look around you. Question the existing situation. This allows you to see things more clearly and be more sensitive to potential problems. Begin by asking yourself, "Why are we doing it this way?" "Is there a better way to do this job?" "Are we causing difficulty to other individuals by doing it this way?"

It is important that you question and examine every existing situation and that you approach each one with the idea that it can be improved.

SOLVING PROBLEMS

Some of you may ask, "Why do we need a process at all? Everyone knows how to solve problems, don't they? After all, it's something we do every day. . . ."

Unfortunately, as we have found out, we often do not solve problems very well, or as well as we could. Most of the time the solutions we generate are only partial or incomplete. Because of this the results are less than satisfactory, even though we tend to view them as O.K. Typical results of incomplete problem solving are as follows:

- Our actions solve only part of the problem, not all of it.
- Sometimes solutions are implemented that actually don't solve the real problem. We may "solve" a problem only to find out that our "solution" had no impact on the problem at hand.
- Sometimes we "solve" a problem in one area, only to find out that we have simply moved it somewhere else.
- Sometimes our "solution" to a problem creates two more problems.

The process I suggest here is designed to help you learn not only how to solve problems logically and systematically but also how to prevent their reoccurrence. We are not going to learn how to apply bandaids to problems or how to put out fires one step ahead of disaster.

Traditionally we seek solutions as quickly as possible, not necessarily the right ones or the best ones, or even a good one, but a solution nonetheless. This approach to problem solving results in the four points listed above. Solutions are seldom long-lasting and tend to mask the real problem for a short period of time, or move it to another area.

The following pitfalls will be avoided when all of the steps of the formal problem-solving process presented here are followed in sequence.

- *Jumping to conclusions.* We assumed we knew the answers before we understood all aspects of the problem.
- *Failure to gather all of the critical information.* Taking shortcuts and failing to analyze all the data.
- *Inability to affect the problem.* Working on problems that we cannot solve because they are outside of our functional area.
- *Working on poorly defined problems.* Typically, these problems are too large, too general, too complicated, or too poorly defined for anyone to solve.
- *Selecting an impractical solution.* The solution selected may be inappropriate because it is too expensive, too time-consuming, unsafe, or, in general terms, unworkable.
- *Failure to involve all the stakeholders.* Failure to involve all of the people impacted by the problem or its solution may cause any attempt to solve it to fail.

- *Lack of planning.* Finding the solution is only half the battle. If we fail to carefully plan proper implementation or evaluate the results of the change, we may settle for less than a complete solution to the problem.
- *Partial, ineffective, or incomplete solutions.* These are often brought on by a complete misunderstanding of the time and resources required to solve the problem.

When these things happen, not only are the original problems unresolved but people become even more frustrated than before! Ineffective problem solving is a waste of time, energy, resources, and effort. It fails to solve the problem at hand, and may even create some new ones.

This text is designed to assist you in developing your problem-solving skills by teaching you the basic principles, procedures, and techniques of problem solving, and how they apply to your job.

The process you are about to learn will provide you with a logical, step-by-step approach. Some of the best ideas and examples available in industry today were used in its development.

THE ADVANTAGES OF A FORMAL PROCESS

- Simplicity. There are only six steps. You may find it awkward at first to use the process in a disciplined way, but you will soon find it a natural and easy method of thinking through your problem.
- Can be used by individuals or groups. When used by a group there are some differences in techniques, but these are easily mastered.
- Can be used at any level of the organization. People at all levels of the organization will find that this process fits in with their decision making. Decisions, large and small, are best made using facts and a logical, step-by-step procedure.
- Provides a common language and approach. This is the key to solving problems. It means you and your group will be able to work with each other more effectively.

DOCUMENT THE PROCESS

Throughout this book you will be reminded to document your decisions and your findings at each of the six steps in the process. Documentation is an essential part of scientific investigation! It provides a focal point and a path to follow as you go forward, and, if necessary, a path by which you can retrace your steps when things don't work. Documentation will also give you the information you need to answer questions about where you are in the process and what has been done to date.

The process begins with a standardized six-page format. I keep these work sheets on my computer and print them as required. Each work sheet covers one step in the problem-solving process, and, if necessary, may serve as an index of all the information you have gathered. The key here is to use these work sheets as you work your way through a problem. Each one relates to a chapter in this text. For example, "Step 1. Identify the Problem" relates to Chapter 3. Now let's look at all the work sheets as we briefly run through the six steps of the problem-solving process.

Step 1. Identify the problem

Date: ________

Identify group members: ______________________________

Problem statement: ______________________________

Contributing factors: ______________________________

Gatekeeping: ______________________________

Goal Statement: ______________________________

Page 1

Identify the Problem

IDENTIFY THE PROBLEM

The first step in the problem-solving process is to determine what is wrong, what might be causing the problem, what you must do to protect the customer, and what you hope to do long-term. Step 1 relates to Chapter 3.

Step 2. Analyze the problem

Describe the action plan: ______

Describe your information requirements: ______

Describe the time required to complete this plan: ______

Page 2

Analyze the Problem

ANALYZE THE PROBLEM

At this stage you will be required to develop your plan of action. As part of this you should determine your information needs and a time to complete. Step 2 relates to Chapter 4.

Step 3. Generate possible solutions

List in detail all possible solutions: ______________________________

Can any of the above be combined? ______________________________

List two or more possible solutions: ______________________________

Page 3

Generate Possible Solutions

GENERATE POSSIBLE SOLUTIONS

Here you will begin to formulate your solutions. Step 3 relates to Chapter 5.

Step 4. Selection

What testing must be done: ________________________________

Does the proposed solution meet all of the criteria? ________________

Has the solution been reviewed with all affected parties? Who are they?

Page 4

The Selection Process

THE SELECTION PROCESS

At this stage, after studying all of the possible solutions, you must select one and justify—either to yourself or to others—your choice. Step 4 relates to Chapter 6.

Step 5. Implement

Describe in detail the implementation plan:

Item	Description of Action Requirements	Who	Completion

Is a detailed timing plan required? (explain):

Page 5

The Implementation Process

THE IMPLEMENTATION PROCESS

At this step in the process you will be required to develop an implementation plan. Step 5 relates to Chapter 7.

Step 6. Measurement

Describe in detail your short-term plan to measure the results:

Was the problem solved? If yes, go to the next step in the process. If no, return to Step one of the problem-solving process, using what you have learned to restate and reevaluate the problem.

Describe in detail your long-term plan to control the process:

Page 6

The Measurement Systems

THE MEASUREMENT SYSTEMS

This is the final step in the process. You will be required to develop a control plan to measure the results of your problem-solving efforts. Step 6 relates to Chapter 8.

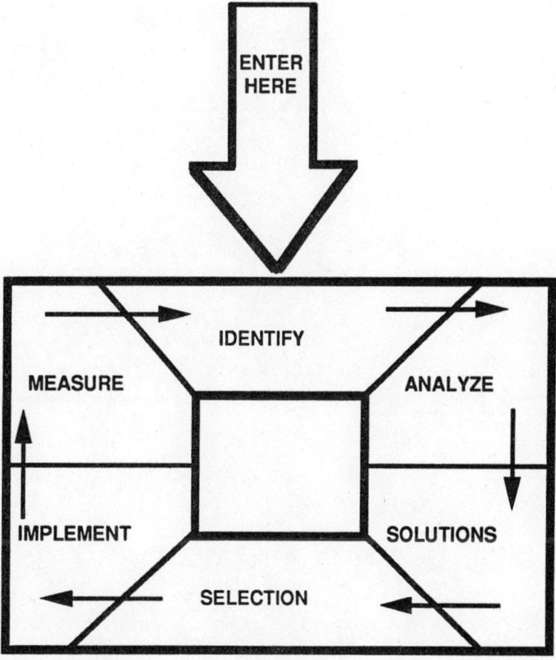

The Six-Step Process

THE PRINCIPLES AND PROCEDURES

The model displayed here represents the six steps, or procedures, of the problem-solving process you are about to learn: Identify, Analyze, Solutions, Selection, Implement, and Measure. These principles form the basis of this process and are the subjects of Chapters 3 through 8. The techniques you will be exposed to in each chapter are the tools you will need to explore your problems each step of the way and bring them to ultimate resolution.

Remember, problem solving is like chemistry or physics. It is a science, but it is not an exact science. Expect that you will make some incorrect assumptions as to the nature of the problem you want to solve. And don't let yourself become frustrated if your solution does not fix the problem immediately and completely. I have found that very few things are ever totally wrong. Most ideas have some merit. In most cases, the work you have done will provide you with a solid platform on which to continue.

Chapter 2

DEFINITION OF THE WORD "PROBLEM"

When we use the word "problem" we should be clear about what we mean. How do we define "problem"?

Webster defines "problem" as an intricate unsettled question, a source of perplexity, a mystery or puzzle. These are all areas or things that can and do present us with a challenge. In fact, many of us enjoy solving mysteries and doing puzzles as a form of relaxation or for the challenge they present to our mind. So, why not carry that challenge into the workplace?

The problem-solving process you are about to learn will assist you in resolving the mysteries and puzzles you face in doing your everyday job.

The fact is, there are many definitions of the word "problem." In industry most of them incorporate the following idea:

> A gap exists between current level of performance and the measured standard for the operation. The standard level of performance is the level required to maintain high customer satisfaction.

In other words, something is not as it should be, or as someone wants it to be. But this is a very broad definition. In practice, there are many different types of problems in business. In the manufacturing environment, they all stem from one or more of the "ingredients" illustrated here. These ingredients—Man, Machine, Method,

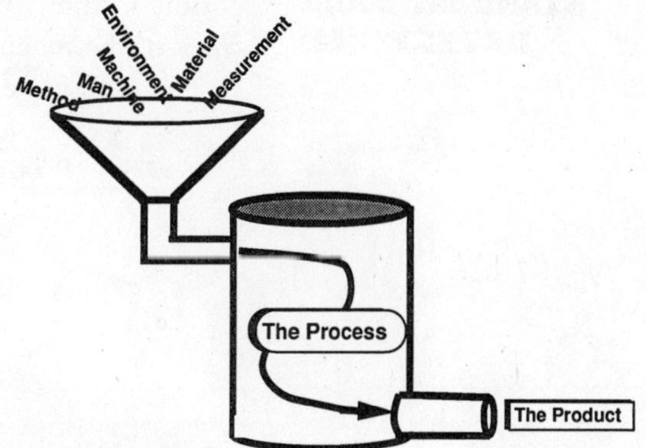

Blending the Key Ingredients

Material, Measurement, and Environment—are the key contributors to any system of accomplishing work. All are mixed together in unequal amounts as part of the process of manufacturing a product. Problems arise when one of these ingredients is poorly formulated or out of balance. We will look at these ingredients again in Chapter 3.

The world we work in tends to believe that any plan—because it is a plan—is perfect, and that therefore the outcome can be nothing less. This, however, is about as far from the truth as you can get. The test of any plan comes during its implementation and not before. Until then, variations should not be viewed as poor planning but as opportunities to solve problems. Problem solving is an ongoing procedure. To put it in perspective, think about what things can change in your workplace day to day.

Before we discuss the types and kinds of problems you may face in the workplace, we need to consider standards of performance, an important contributor to the problem-solving process.

PERFORMANCE STANDARDS

What is a performance standard? To assist us in defining what a performance standard is, let's look at what it is not. Performance standards are not goals, they are not peaks which you hit periodically, and they are not what someone feels something is capable of doing.

Some people have a great deal of trouble differentiating a goal from a standard. Goals are what you need to improve current level of performance to solve "anticipated" problems. Later in this chapter you will read about the "anticipated" problem.

Now let's look at what a performance standard is.

A performance standard is the average performance of a person or process, measured over time.

What can performance standards do for you? Basically, they tell you if you have a problem. This is because the information they provide is the minimum you need to diagnose your problem.

HOW PERFORMANCE STANDARDS ARE DETERMINED

For example, say Company X has purchased a new machine to make outlets in their pump line. The employees in the department kept track of the machine output for the first 28 days of operation.

The data are as follows:

Day	*Production Count*	*Day*	*Production Count*
1	200	15	260
2	180	16	235
3	135	17	271
4	156	18	311
5	167	19	243
6	146	20	289
7	168	21	341

Day	*Production Count*	*Day*	*Production Count*
8	171	22	256
9	104	23	375
10	236	24	271
11	302	25	339
12	289	26	354
13	201	27	306
14	278	28	342

To determine the performance standard for the first 28 days of operation, total the output for that period and divide by the number of days worked (28). In our example, the total number of units produced was 6926. If we divide that by the number of days worked we find that our standard level of performance for the first 28 days was 247.35 units per day (the average). Let's look at that result graphically in Performance Standards (A).

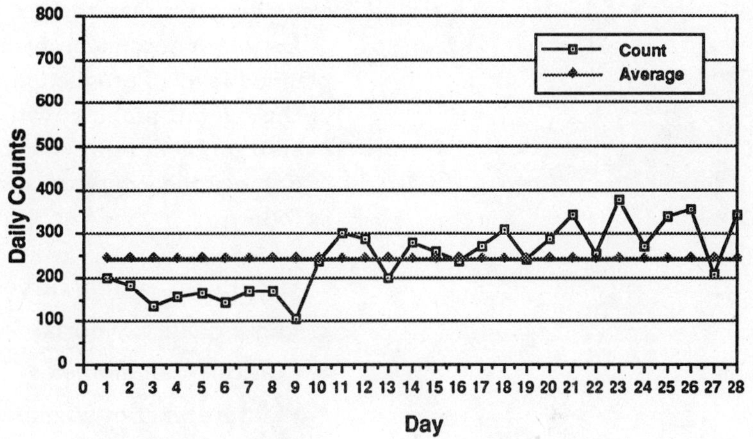

Performance Standards (A)

The graph also shows us that what we have experienced is normal variation during the first 28 days of operation. As you can see, the daily output for the first nine days of operation was averaged at approximately 150 units per day. At this point something changed—different tools, new fixture details, etc.—which helped raise the daily average. In addition, we see that we have a trend: that is, we are improving with time. It is important to identify such changes and how they affect a system or process in either a positive or negative manner. The effects are all part of the problem-solving process.

By adding another line to this graph we can visualize our goal, that is, where we must be in order to meet customer demand on this piece of equipment, as measured against current level of perfor-

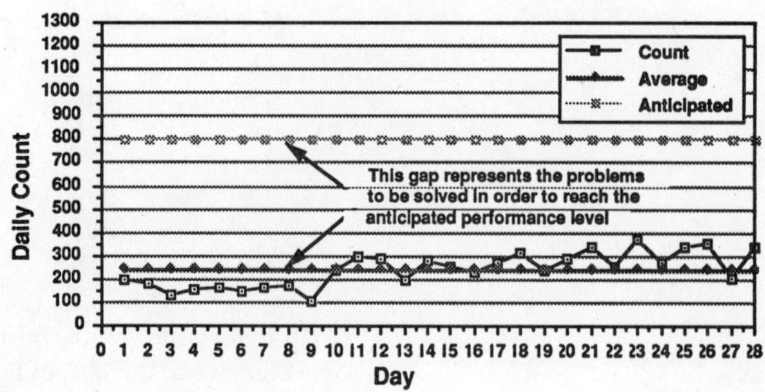

Performance Standards (B)

mance (see Performance Standards (B)). The difference between the two lines—average and the anticipated—represents the problems that must be solved in order to reach the planned level of performance. If we are unable to solve these problems, then the real performance standard for this piece of equipment might become something less than the planned production rate.

Let's look at some problems that could stop you from reaching the planned level of production. To identify which of these is at the root of the overall problem will require you to thoroughly analyze the overall problem using the six-step process.

Some of the symptoms of poor performance for machine tools are as follows:

- Operator learning curve
- Poor-quality material
- Cutting-tool problems
- Fixture wear or alignment
- Worn locators
- Variation in air pressure
- Variation in hydraulic pressure
- Worn fixture details
- Change in suppliers for tools or materials
- Change in the process (upstream)
- Engineering change in product
- Etc.

These are all said to be *assignable causes of a variation to the normal process*. Relate these back to Performance Standards (A), which has us in a start-up mode. These kinds of problems are typical of those that must be solved to achieve the planned rate.

The difference between goals and standards becomes more clear when we look at Performance Standards (C). In this graph we see

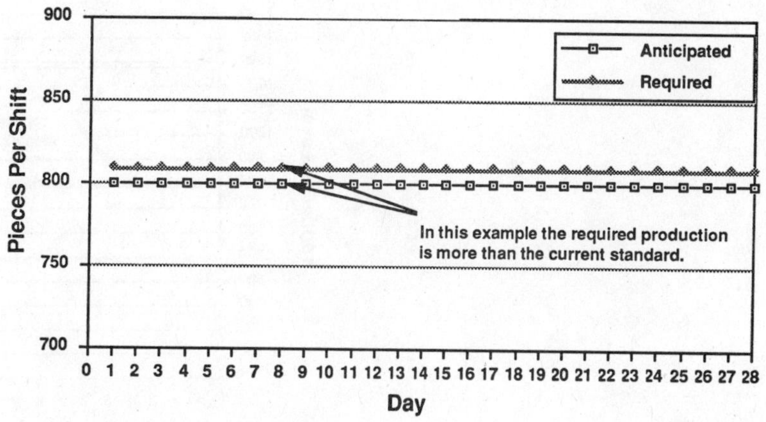

Performance Standards (C)

that the process has a *performance standard* of 756 units per shift. In order to meet the current demand for the product, the *goal* is to increase the output per shift of 756 units by 80 pieces—to 836 units. The difference between the current level and the goal may represent one or two large problems or several small ones. You will learn the process necessary to identify and solve these problems.

WHY PERFORMANCE STANDARDS ARE REQUIRED

Everybody likes to know how they are doing. Performance standards allow you to track your progress, or lack of it. Performance standards are at the heart of a sound problem-solving process because you must know where you are before you can begin planning for the future.

Imagine a golfer who never kept score or who never maintained his average. If this man were to go out and spend a lot of money on lessons to improve his game, it would be extremely difficult for him to measure the value of the lessons. To develop your business plan you need to know your current level of performance and what constitutes a normal operation level.

Knowing how your business is performing allows you to accurately determine the cost structure of your business. Knowing how you are doing also tells you what you must do to improve your performance. Ultimately this will determine your ability to stay in business. The real benefit, however, of charting performance is that it makes it easy to visualize progress.

PERFORMANCE STANDARDS AND CONTINUOUS IMPROVEMENT

Remember, performance standards remain constant under normal operating conditions. The key word is "standard." Standard of performance is not engineered performance, current performance, or required performance. These are defined as follows:

- *Engineered performance* is the gross cycle time of a machine or operation. From a problem-solving perspective, the gap between current and engineered standards represents the problem. Clos-

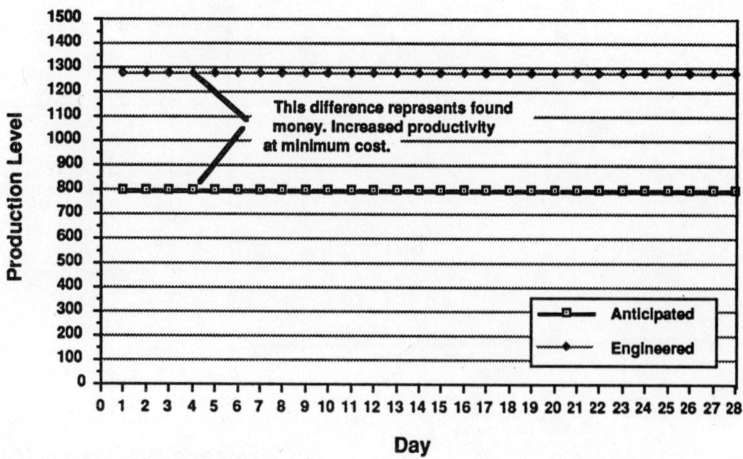

Performance Standards (D)

ing the gap (solving the problem) represents increased capacity and lower cost to a business at a minimum investment level.

- *Current performance* may be greater or less than standard performance. If greater, it would be nice to know how the improvements were accomplished so that they could be standardized. Conversely, if current performance is less than standard, it should send an alarm that something has changed, and the operation must be brought back to its standard level of performance.
- *Required performance* can vary from the operational standards in both positive and negative directions. If a business has a standard level of performance of 100 pieces per hour, and the required demand for the product is currently 125 pieces per hour, this business must determine how to meet the current requirement.

These three kinds of performance levels have one thing in common: they offer, to either the individual or the group involved, opportunities to solve problems. Standard performance levels offer a means of measuring success.

PROBLEM TYPES

The ability to sort out problems will enable you to decide how much and what kinds of resources and efforts will be involved in solving them. To assist you, I have determined four types of problems you might be faced with. The following paragraphs explain the four types. These types are based on the individual's ability to directly influence the outcome, as well as the amount of effort required to solve the problem.

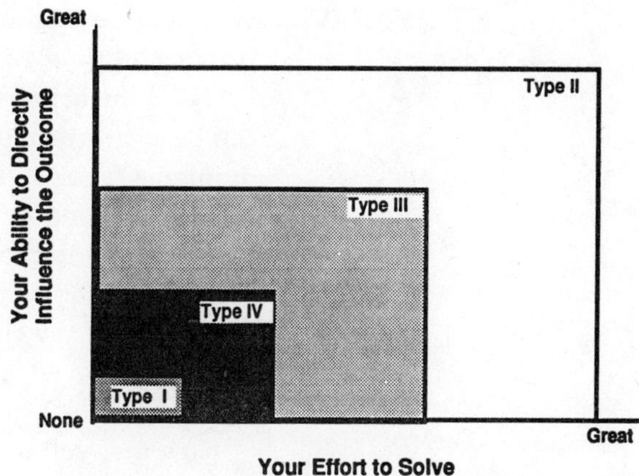

TYPE I When faced with a Type I problem, an individual or a small group will have little or no ability to effect a solution. An example of this type of problem might be world peace, something to strive for but—as an individual or small group—we know our ability to influence those in charge of making it happen is minimal. Another example might be the drug problem in America, or rumors in the workplace. These are the problems we are faced with every day in the newspapers we read. These are the problems that make for interesting conversation but that in reality we can impact the least. The unfortunate part is that we tend to spend a great deal of time talking about these kinds of problems.

TYPE II With a Type II problem, the individual or small group involved has the responsibility, authority, and skills required to make the changes necessary to solve the problem they have identified. Examples of this type of problem are poor departmental housekeeping, poor departmental quality, and low productivity in the department. All of these problems are best addressed by those who do the job daily.

TYPE III The individual or small group faced with a Type III problem finds that they have only partial responsibility or authority to make the changes required to solve the problem, or that the skills necessary to make the changes are not available inside the work group. An example of this type of problem might involve the cooperation of two production departments to solve a quality problem in Department B. In this example, Department A supplies Department B with the materials it needs to produce the finished product. Department B is generating unusually high levels of scrap and rework, and the problem has been traced to the process in Department A. To solve this problem and ensure the product quality, individuals from Departments A and B must work together.

TYPE IV

With a Type IV problem the individual or group is charged with the responsibility of reporting that a problem exists, but must rely entirely on the actions of others to solve the problem. Examples of this can be seen when product engineering changes are required to solve problems found in the marketplace or the workplace. The problem is reported, and at this point the engineers must make the changes they feel will improve the product's quality, either on the shop floor or in the dealer showroom. The key here is that you can only monitor the results of the change and report back your findings. You are not directly involved.

Now that you understand the types of problems you will be faced with, let's look at another category of problems—kinds of problems.

KINDS OF PROBLEMS

There are at least four major different kinds of problems: policy, technical, process, and people.

POLICY PROBLEMS

Policy problems are the kinds of problems that arise from the policies, rules, and so on of your organization. For example, your company has decided to move the starting time of the first shift from 7:00 A.M. to 6:00 A.M. on Monday of next week. The women working on the first shift are concerned because none of the child-care facilities in the area are open before 6:30 A.M. Other kinds of problems that fall in this arena are work rules, medical coverage, vacation time off, and employee benefits.

TECHNICAL PROBLEMS

Technical problems are the kinds of problems that involve defective equipment or machine breakdowns. For example, the machine line you are working seems to be breaking down on a regular basis ever since the new materials-handling system was installed. All of the breakdowns seem to be attributed to electrical problems that occur between the handling system and your machine. Upon further investigation you find that the computer that operates the handling system and that controls the machine cycle has a cracked circuitboard. The board functions properly until it heats up, then the circuit opens and causes the machine to malfunction. The time required to repair the damage is usually long enough to allow the board to cool down and operate properly.

Other problems that would fall in this category are materials-handling components that periodically drop parts, machines that have high levels of downtime, frequent failure of the same mechanical/electrical component part, and groups of similar machines that have the same problems.

PROCESS PROBLEMS

Process problems are the kinds of problems that involve the methods you use to manufacture the parts. They involve the way jobs are being done or how things are working. For example, several workstations on the assembly line were rearranged recently to improve the product quality. The assembly sequence was changed and the work reallocated between the stations. The workstation where a hydraulic pump is assembled to the main assembly can no longer keep up with the cycle of the line. Upon investigation it was found that the employee at the pump assembly station was overallocated, and that by moving some of the subassembly operation on the hydraulic pump to another workstation the assembler was able to keep up. Other examples of process problems are gage repeatability, poor tool life, difficult or time-consuming changeovers, tool-setting problems, assembly problems, quality problems, and so forth.

PEOPLE PROBLEMS

People problems are the kinds of problems that involve the behavior of, or relationships between, individuals. These can be difficult problems to solve and in some cases should be left to professionals. I have found that problems of this kind are usually due to a poorly trained employee or one who does not understand his or her role in the organization. Fortunately, these can be easily corrected. Other issues might involve substance abuse, i.e., drugs or alcohol. These, once identified, are best left to the professionals.

EXERCISE

Referring to the four categories above, identify the kinds of problems represented by the following examples:

- The business you work for has changed the retirement plan for the workers.
- The machines in your area seem to be unable to produce a part that is of consistent quality.
- It has become very frustrating to try and maintain the level of product quality necessary to keep your company's product competitive in the marketplace.
- The gages that you must work with don't give consistent readings.
- The employee on the next operation seems to be absent from work quite a bit. When he is, the quality of the product suffers.
- The company has decided to relocate a portion of its operation to another plant. This will make your daily drive twice as long as it is currently.
- The light in your work area blinks on and off during the day. When this happens the equipment you are working on does not always do what it is supposed to do.
- The final assembly line in your area has been rearranged to add a new part. The problem is that you must now work twice as hard to assemble the old part numbers.

- You suspect that the employee working on the machine next to you has a drug problem. The employee's current work habits at times endanger the safety of other employees.

Another way of classifying problems is to describe them by the *way* they happen; that is, problems can occur unexpectedly, or they may be anticipated.

PROBLEMS CAN BE UNEXPECTED OR ANTICIPATED

Many problems occur inadvertently. No one intends them or expects them to happen. These *unexpected problems* are what people think of when they hear the word "problem." Here is an example of an unexpected or unintended problem:

The machine you are working on was purchased to produce 1400 quality parts during an eight-hour shift; to date its output is averaging 1000 parts per shift. The problem in this case is to identify all of the causes that must be corrected to ensure that 1400 quality parts are produced every eight hours. Once these possible causes have been identified, the next step is to determine which ones can be removed from your list. This is done by testing and experimentation. Some of the factors identified can be directly influenced by the operators (Type II or III problems); others will require help (Type I and IV problems).

In this situation, the goal of problem solving is to bring actual production levels up to the standards that have been established.

Some problems, however, are intentionally created and should be identified as *anticipated problems*. Expected, or anticipated, problems require that new performance standards be set. The existing levels of performance must be reviewed and new ones established. Then all possible problems that might stop you from accomplishing your new goals must be anticipated and solved prior to system start-up. Here is an example of an anticipated problem:

The production for this system has been 1400 units every eight hours (the standard), but customer demand has gone up to 1500 per shift (new standard). In this situation, the goal of problem solving is to find a way of meeting the new standard in the most quality-minded and cost-effective manner.

There is yet another way of describing a problem—by its size or degree of urgency.

SIZE AND URGENCY OF A PROBLEM

Problems come in all sizes and degrees of urgency. Some problems by their very nature can be solved right away. Others may not represent a major problem now, but could become one in the future.

Here is an example of an urgent problem

One of the machines in your department has a history of developing an oil leak once or twice a year. For the last couple of weeks it has been almost impossible to keep oil in the machine. In order to avoid a catastrophe the machine must be fixed now. In this case the machine's oil leak grew from a periodic annoyance to what could have been a major production-stopping breakdown had it not been shut down and repaired.

Here is an example of a potential problem

Work in one of your assembly areas has not been up to standard, but everyone in the area is skilled and there are no problems because of lack of job instructions. However, when new employees join the work group there may be a problem with quality or safety. In this case we should look at how new employees are trained. It could be that a formal on-the-job training program would avoid these kinds of problems.

We must become aware of the fact that what today may seem unimportant can quickly grow into something that has the potential of stopping the entire production system, or, in the case of quality problems, affecting the customer's willingness to buy.

EXERCISE Using the descriptions and examples, identify the following as either urgent or potential. While you're at it, describe the potential size of the problem.

- The product you are manufacturing is losing sales at the rate of 4 percent per year. After some study the problem looks like the decline in market is due to poor quality.
- Housekeeping in your department has been on a downhill slide. Some of it is due to poor personal habits, that is, people throwing things on the floor. Some is due to oils and coolants running out onto the floor.
- Your business is seasonal; demand for your products comes in the spring and early summer. It is January and you are making only 60 percent of what you are capable of producing.

WHO'S RESPONSIBLE FOR SOLVING PROBLEMS?

An important ingredient of any company is that every member of the organization has the responsibility to identify problems and to participate in their solution. Some problems, of course, are so complex, or affect so many different people or sections, that they must be solved by a group or team working together every step of the way.

Others may be worked on by one or two people—at least in the beginning stages. Even when you feel that you have both the responsibility and the authority to solve a specific problem, you will find that most problems will be solved better and faster with the assistance and cooperation of others. One way of determining who might help you in solving your problem is to develop a resource chart such as the one illustrated here. There can be drawbacks to developing a resource chart. The two that come to mind are:

- You may identify someone as a resource who is unable to help.
- You may get the runaround from people who don't want to get involved.

Department: ______________ **Date:** ________

Problem Identified:

Resource	**Service Supplied**
Name: Company: Ph#. Address:	
Name: Company: Ph#. Address:	
Name: Company: Ph#. Address:	
Name: Company: Ph#. Address:	
Name: Company: Ph#. Address:	

The way to handle these situations is to ask!

The real reason for developing a chart like this is to better understand what is going on around you. The key to developing the chart itself is to write down in one place all of the names of those who can assist you in solving your problems, and how to contact them.

Moreover, involving other people in the problem-solving process has many advantages:

- We are more creative in developing ideas about solutions when we work with other people.

- We help ensure our ability to get approval to implement the solutions we have identified.
- The solutions themselves are implemented more effectively because those affected have participated in developing them, understand them, and are committed to them.

In other words, the most effective problem-solving effort is one that involves all of the stakeholders.

EXERCISE Develop a resource chart for the area you are currently working in. Remember, list everyone who affects your job. If you don't know, ask.

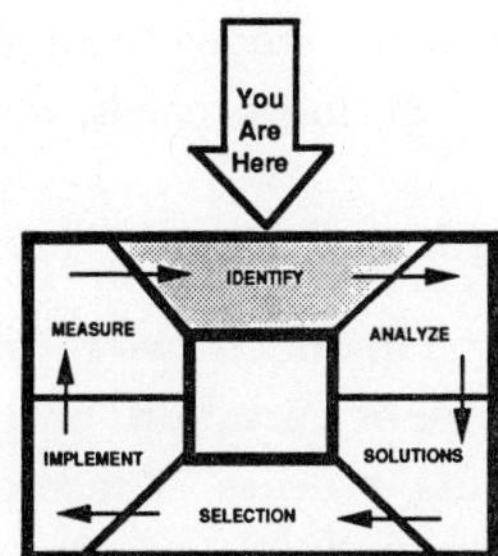

Chapter 3

PROBLEM IDENTIFICATION OR SELECTION

In the problem identification/selection phase of this problem-solving process, it is essential that you collect sufficient data before you begin. Having the facts will assist you or your group in determining what kinds of administrative controls are necessary to ensure that nothing but high-quality parts reach your customer.

IDENTIFY THE PROBLEM OR AREA FOR IMPROVEMENT

You may be given a problem to work on, or sometimes a group is asked or directed to work on a specific problem by their supervisor. In this case, the problem is usually within their specific area of responsibility. Individuals are often brought together as a task force to work on a problem that is broad in scope and too complex for one person alone.

Sometimes, however, you may be able to choose for yourself the problem you want to work on. You may want to work on it alone, or you may feel more comfortable, the first time around, as a member of a group. In either case, the first step is to define the problem. *Remember, for the first one, choose a type of problem that you or the members of your group have control over.* Don't choose a Type I problem like world peace because your ability to impact the outcome is minimal. The first principle of this process—to identify the problem—is designed to assist you in choosing a problem that you will be able to work on and to solve. The question we ask ourselves is, "What is it that we want to change, or What needs to be improved?"

To identify areas for improvement, you need to have a clear idea of what you really want to see happen in your workplace. You need to understand the current situation and why it needs to be changed. In our everyday lives we take so many actions without a clear goal in mind that we sometimes do not consciously know what outcome we really want to achieve. When goals are unclear, undefined, or inappropriate, then actions will be inappropriate, causing confusion or misdirection. Once goals become clear, problems and actions required to solve them become visible also. The key to everyday improvement or problem solving is clarity, clarity of the situation and then what must be done to correct it.

In this chapter we will investigate the steps required to work with the first principle of this problem-solving process, identification of the problem you will work on.

MANAGING THE UNEXPECTED PROBLEM

Manufacturing problems come to us in one of two forms: they either have an assignable, or special, cause of variation, or there are problems inherent in the manufacturing process. These are said to be chronic problems. A manufacturing problem can come in the form of an unexpected occurrence, or be selected by you as something that is chronic and long overdue to be fixed.

To manage the unexpected problem, more commonly known as "the surprise," you will need to know some of its possible sources within the manufacturing process, and to work through the possible situations to better understand the process and techniques of problem solving.

As explained in Chapter 2, the unexpected problem normally arises from an unanticipated source in the manufacturing process. Some part of the manufacturing process has been neglected, or allowed to function in an unmanaged manner. For example,

- Failure to regularly change tools
- Neglected quality procedures
- Poorly maintained fixtures
- Inconsistent assembly practices
- Poorly maintained machines
- Inaccurate gages
- Incapable machines

This type of system failure is said to have an *assignable* cause. It is normally due to

- Missing or shallow drilled holes
- Drilled holes that are not tapped
- Oversize or undersize holes
- Mating parts that won't go together
- Fluid or air leaks in assemblies
- Frequent machine failures
- Surface finish problems

These problems are usually found and solved in the manufacturing stage. However, sometimes resultant poor-quality parts find their way into the hands of customers. To manage these unexpected problems the following procedure should be used.

IDENTIFY

Unexpected problems usually come in the form of a telephone call. "You had better get over here, we have a problem." These problems are easy to find because they cause normal daily operations to stop. An example would be:

The tool that finish bores the oil pump pocket was missed during the normal tool change cycle. Because of this oversight the parts made all had gear pockets that were undersize. These parts were found in final assembly when the operator tried to assemble the pumps.

Unfortunately, this is how a lot of problems in our manufacturing process are found. These are the problems that have an assignable cause—in this case the worn boring tool. You do not, however, know why the worn tool was left in the machine.

ASSESS THE MAGNITUDE

In this step you will assess the extent of the problem. When the problem is found it is essential that the manufacturing process be stopped and all of the out-of-specification parts found. This will help you to evaluate the size of the problem and will give you time to think about some possible immediate solutions. Remember to look off-line as well as on-line for the parts. If yours is a typical operation, look in all of your off-line storage areas, banks, repair areas, and so forth. It is important that you find all of the poor-quality material.

IMMEDIATE FIX

To resume operation, an immediate fix is what must be done. In the case of our undersize gear pockets example, two alternatives might be:

- Repair all of the existing pumps now so that they can be used.
- Remove all the pumps found in the containment phase from the area and refill the system with dimensionally good material.

Remember, the objective of any manufacturing system is to provide high-quality parts to the customer. This step in the process ensures an uninterrupted supply of material to the customer, but it must not be viewed as the final solution. To ensure the problem is solved you must work through the entire process.

GATEKEEPING

Until you have worked the problem through the entire process it is necessary to take some sort of short-term action to ensure no repeat of the current problem. The gatekeeping activity might involve the operator making periodic checks of the operation. This would ensure you are not having abnormal tool wear. Another activity might involve checking all of the parts at the point of build. The purpose of the gatekeeping activity is to provide short-term assurance of quality. One of the more effective methods of gatekeeping is to establish a visual signaling system.

One of the more frequently used systems is the *problem board.* The problem board can be something simple like a large sheet of paper, laid out as shown here.

Departmental Problem Resolution Information Board			
Number	Description	Assign to:	Promised Date

The problem board is a communication tool. All of the employees who work in the area are kept aware of what is happening. The typical column headers you will find on these boards are a problem identification number, Problem Statement, assigned to:, anticipated completion, and last updated. When the problem is solved it is removed from the board and the documentation filed by subject or operation. The purpose of this is to establish a history file of problems and their solutions.

The key to the problem board's effectiveness is the discipline of using it. Many people will avoid using a tool like this for the simple reason that once their name is on the board they are accountable.

There are other methods I have seen for keeping a problem visible. Two of these are as follows:

- A list of all questionable operations and materials is displayed at plant entrances. If employees have prior knowledge, then major problems can be averted. Awareness will bring about the efforts necessary to improve the process.
- Signs similar to stop signs are placed where problems have been identified. The only way these signs can be removed from the area is when the problem-solving process has been completed and the problem resolved. Each sign represents one problem.

Visual management is limited only by your imagination and your willingness to let people know that you have a problem. Remember, one of the reasons for maintaining a high level of visibility is to solicit the ideas of others.

COMMUNICATE

"Communication" is the most overused word in the language of the American businessperson. In industry, we don't have a communications problem, we just have a bunch of people who don't want to talk to each other. It is important to establish an environment in which people feel comfortable talking about things that are not as they should be. This kind of environment takes time to develop.

Communication in the problem-solving process is essential. Essential because, in this phase of the process, the operation needs to minimize the time between the stop and start of production. The steps in communication are:

- Communicate that there is a problem.
- Communicate what the problem is.
- Communicate the scope of the problem.
- Communicate the possible solutions.
- Communicate any change of status.
- Communicate the gatekeeper activity.
- Communicate who is responsible for the follow-up.

When dealing with problems that have an assignable cause, it is important to let people know what is happening. It is important to let the organization know that there is a problem and, what is even more important, to submit status reports until the problem has been solved.

CONTINUOUS IMPROVEMENT

Working on problems in this mode is different from the process described for dealing with the unexpected problem. Here you will be dealing with problems that have been around for a long time. These problems may be so deeply seated in your business that they have become part of the operating budget. It is important to have good information when dealing with these problems.

How many times have you said, or heard someone else say,

- "When figuring out the production schedule, make a 40 percent allowance for machine downtime."
- "When you order material for that department, put in an additional 30 percent for scrap."
- "When you figure the production lead times for that department, their historical performance says to add 25 percent to your estimated times."

Statements like these indicate that your business has accepted these conditions as the standard of performance for your business. Accepting them will only add to the costs of doing business, costs that will reduce operating profits and money used for raises or costs that must be passed along to the customer, making your product or service noncompetitive.

Ongoing problems can be found at all levels of your business, and relate directly to the cost and quality of the goods and services offered by any business. Some places to start looking for these problems are:

- Departmental scrap reports
- Departmental repair records
- Customer complaints
- Warranty data
- Machine downtime records
- Late or missed shipments
- Low acceptance levels at inspection
- Repetitive failure of the process
- Etc.

When you work on these kinds of problems you are improving your company's ability to compete and survive in today's market.

ANALYZING THE WORKPLACE

Exploring the workplace is another method of identifying problems. Too often you accept how the workplace is laid out and how the job gets done as the best or only way of performing the tasks. How many times have you told yourself, "If only they had asked me."

First, take a global approach to the problem. Visualize what you are doing.

- Think about what you must do in order to perform your job.
- Identify non-value-added activities.

Ask yourself what is the sequence of events, and the flow of work.

- Organize the work events in the order that you perform them.
- Recognize how work flows through your department.
- Recognize how your workstation fits into the whole process.

Identify bottlenecks in the flow.

- Look for excessive material build-up ahead of operations.
- Look for workers in the department who never get done.
- Look for operations that are always waiting for material.

Work with other employees in your area if possible. The real strength of analyzing the workplace is to get all of the parties involved in working on the problem. The solutions will be better, and will carry a higher level of acceptance.

Second, analyze your individual workstation. The steps used are similar to those used in the global approach just described. The real difference here is that you now have your own workstation under the microscope. To better understand what you do and how you accomplish your tasks, do the following:

- Flowchart what you do in your own job.
- Break the chart down into small, measurable units.
- Analyze the relationship of each small unit to all the other units.
- Find the areas where *improvements* can be made.

To accomplish your goals,

- Identify the *ideal* level of performance in each small unit.
- Identify the *existing* level of performance in each small unit.
- Assess the difference between the two. Your problem-solving activities should be centered around closing the gap between the ideal and the current level of performance.

There are many tools that can help us analyze our workplace to identify problems. Some of the more useful ones will be described with examples shown either in the text or in the "tool chest" at the end of this chapter.

GENERATE AND LIST IDEAS

The most effective method of generating ideas for improvement is to have the team members sit down and make a list of the areas in the workplace they feel need improving. This is a very powerful tactic; the number of viewpoints and perspectives offered will only enhance the process. When working in groups, the major problem you will encounter is keeping them focused on the problem at hand. You will also be faced with the differences in personalities, and do they or don't they fit. If this group is going to work together at all it must establish some group norms. Such norms might include:

- Being polite to each other.
- Agreeing to disagree (friendly disagreement).
- How decisions will be made.
- Who will chair the meeting.
- Etc.

No one knows the problems associated with a job or task better than the person expected to perform it daily. This person is the real expert and the best source of ideas for improvement.

To generate ideas, try to identify as many problems as you can and write them down. This is the thinking process. If you are working in a group, get everyone to participate. One excellent way of accomplishing this is called *brainstorming*. Brainstorming is a method used in groups to get everyone involved in generating ideas; literally, an "idea storm." There are three main techniques for facilitating a brainstorming session.

- ***Freewheeling.*** Everyone shouts out their ideas as they think of them. The ideas are written on a flip chart by the group leader or facilitator.
- ***Round Robin.*** People take turns giving their ideas, or "pass" if they do not have an idea on this round. When everyone has passed in one round of the group the brainstorming is over. All the ideas are written on a flip chart.
- ***Slip Method.*** People write their ideas down on paper and give them to the group or team leader to write on a flip chart. This is a good technique to use if people are too inhibited to express their ideas out loud.

Brainstorming allows you to generate as many ideas as possible—and to encourage creative thinking. To accomplish this there are some simple rules that must be followed.

- Clearly identify what subject you are working on. It is helpful to write the subject on a large sheet of paper and hang it where it is visible to all of the participants. This is an old technique used to keep the group focused.
- Write down all of the ideas. It is important that you capture everyone's thoughts. You must agree at the outset of the session that there will be no dumb or silly ideas expressed. To accomplish this your group must not criticize any idea. It is extremely important that no one makes a comment or attempts to judge the value of another team member's idea during the brainstorming session.
- Set a time limit for the session. This is important because it assists the facilitator in keeping the group focused. A time limit should be agreed to by the group prior to the start of the session. 5 to 20 minutes is normally a reasonable amount of time.
- Build on each other's ideas. This is an important feature. Most participants come to the session with different levels of knowledge on a given subject.

- When the list is completed, the ideas can be discussed and clarified.

EXERCISE Using the space provided below, develop a list of all of the problems in your work area (this can be done individually or as a group):

BREAK SUBJECTS DOWN TO A WORKABLE SIZE

When you have finished compiling your first list, examine it. Chances are good that whether you are working individually or in a group, you have listed some very large areas. Now it is necessary to break large problems down into small ones and to get a little more specific.

For example, one problem on your list may be "poor attendance." But this topic is too broad for you to effectively solve it. Ask yourself or your group, "What does this mean?" To do this, first break the problem down to all contributing causes. In the case of our example, your list of possible contributing causes might look like this:

- Age of the work force
- Drug abuse
- Double-income families
- Lack of worker involvement in the business
- Etc.

Of all potential causes of "poor attendance" listed, the only two problems that a group might be able to solve or have any impact on are the lack of involvement in the business and drug abuse. It would be fruitless to work on the others, which are impossible to solve. A cause-and-effect diagram might be helpful at this stage (see the section on fishbone, or cause-and-effect diagrams in Chapter 4).

COMBINE ITEMS INTO A PRELIMINARY LIST

When the large problems have been broken down into more manageable small ones, review and combine closely related items together. If you have been working individually, you may not need to spend much time doing this. But if you have been working in a group, you will find out during the brainstorming process that the important thing is to be clear on items that others do not understand. The list can then be reduced by eliminating duplication, or by combining items that are close in meaning. You now have a preliminary list of problems from which to choose.

REDUCE A PRELIMINARY LIST TO A SHORT LIST

If many problems have been identified, it will be necessary to get the list down to a manageable level (three or four items) from which the final selection can be made.

How is this best done? The best way is to consider each problem by asking the following questions:

- Does it really matter whether this problem is solved?
- What is the payback in solving it?
- Is the problem under my or the team's control to solve?
- Is the problem urgent?
- What will happen if it's not solved?
- What are the resources required (time, people, money, materials) to solve the problem?

When you look at each of the problems on your list in light of these questions, you will be able to eliminate some right away, and you will be able to identify which are the most important ones of those that remain.

If you are working in a group, discuss each of the ideas on the list, in turn, in light of these "filter" questions. You may also want to take a preliminary vote about which items stay in active consideration and which do not. For example, if you are in a group of six people, you could say that only items that get four or more votes would stay on the list of possible problems to select. This method can be helped considerably by having available to the group sufficient information relative to potential savings in effort or dollars.

EXERCISE Using the rules you have just learned, break down and combine the items you wrote down on your problem list:

PROBLEM STATEMENTS

Once you have identified the top three or four problems, clarify them by writing a short Problem Statement for each.

Note that it is extremely important to define the problem as well and as accurately as you can. This will ensure a clear understanding of the goal or reason for solving the problem you have identified to work on. It will also assist you in identifying where you must go in order to bring about resolution.

Good Problem Statements describe the current situation in

measurable and *specific* terms about the subject of the problem. Here are some examples of good Problem Statements:

- Defect rates are increasing in the pump line.
- High percentage of assembly line employees are not coming to work.
- Tooling costs are over budget.
- Abnormal number of lost time accidents are occurring.

In each statement we know what the problem is about: the defect rate, attendance, tooling costs, and accident rates. And we know something about what is happening: the on-line defect rate is *too high,* the cost of tooling is *over the budget,* the accident rate is at an *abnormal number,* and the absence rate is *increasing.*

EXERCISE Select a problem from the list that you or your group developed. In the space provided, develop a Problem Statement.

Problem Statement: ______________________________

____

____

____

____

____

____

____

GOAL STATEMENTS

When we write a Goal Statement it is equally important to be clear, concise, accurate, and measurable. The goal should return you to a standard performance level or be formulated to move your organization to a new level of performance.

Goals should force you to reach out of your comfort zone, but not so far that your vision becomes a nightmare. We too often set goals because they will make us look or sound good to others, or they are established when the whole situation is not clearly understood. Goals set under these conditions will only hinder the problem-solving process.

If you are uncertain of the cause of the problem or of your own capabilities, it may be smarter to state your own goal in incremental steps. Each step can then be worked through as a separate problem, and when this process is completed it will add up to a total solution. Working in this manner will allow for some early successes. This method also allows the problem solvers to learn more about the process. These experiences will help in the later goal steps.

If there are currently no standards for performance in question, you may have to define the standard to be achieved. This can be done by considering the following:

- What historically has been your performance level?
- What performance level is being achieved by others doing comparable work?
- What are the organization's current objectives?
- What is necessary now—or what will be needed in the future?

In all cases, the discrepancy that exists (which is the problem) can only be analyzed and brought to resolution if the goal is understood.

EXERCISE

Now that you have identified the problem, what do you want to do with it? In the space provided below define what the situation will look like when you are through working on it.

Goal Statement: ____

____

____

____

____

____

____

____

____

____

____

____

SELECT A PROBLEM

If you are working individually, it is important that selection of the one problem you will work on be done in consultation with your supervisor. First, work out for yourself which one you think would be the best one to tackle. If you are working in a group, it is important that selection be done by reaching a consensus. Consensus is defined below.

How will you make your final selection? There are many ways of reaching this decision. By writing your problem and goal statements, you may have clarified the relative importance of the problems that were left on your short list. It may now be apparent that one of them clearly outweighs all others. If, however, the picture is not clear, you must do some further analysis and thinking.

One method is to compare each item on your short list to every other item, using specific criteria such as control, importance, difficulty, payback, and resources. A way of doing this is to use the Problem Spider (see page 45). In a group, this tool is extremely useful. Group members must assign a numerical rating for each problem on the short list and discuss each problem in light of the rating criteria. This is an excellent way of developing greater consensus.

You may want to consult other people and get their opinion. Choosing the problem to work on is a critical decision. Do not do so in a hurry. Take whatever time is needed—particularly if you are working in a group. Only by taking the time to get consensus can you be sure that you will have a group committed to work on the chosen problem.

When you have identified the problem you believe is the most important to work on, consult with your supervisor in order to confirm your selection and to get agreement on the goal of solving that particular problem.

CONSENSUS: WHAT IS IT?

The best way to describe the consensus style of decision making is by first describing the autocratic and democratic styles, and their advantages and disadvantages.

AUTOCRATIC STYLE

An autocratic organization can best be described by how they communicate with the work force. In the autocratic communication method, as illustrated here, communication is all in one direction, and that is how things are done in this type of organization.

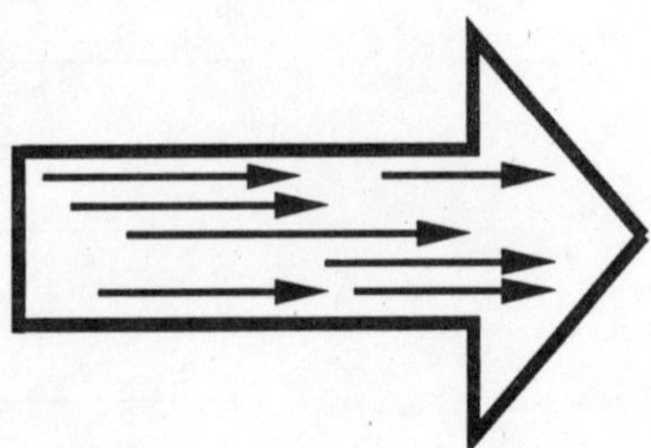

As you can see, all information flows one way, that is, down into the organization, with little or no information flowing in the opposite direction. There are some distinct advantages and disadvantages that go with this style of management. The advantages are as follows:

- Decisions can be made quickly.
- There is no need to consult others.

Disadvantages include:

- One winner and a whole bunch of losers.
- The decision maker must "know it all."

- Lack of acceptance.
- There are times when coercion must be used to reinforce the decision.

It has been my experience that most people will avoid doing what they do not agree with. The real disadvantage is that the business or department will never get any better than that one individual's ability.

DEMOCRATIC STYLE

It is this style that we are most familiar with. We accept the democratic process as a fair and effective method of settling issues, issues such as who will the leader of your team be, who will our next president be, should taxes be raised, and so forth.

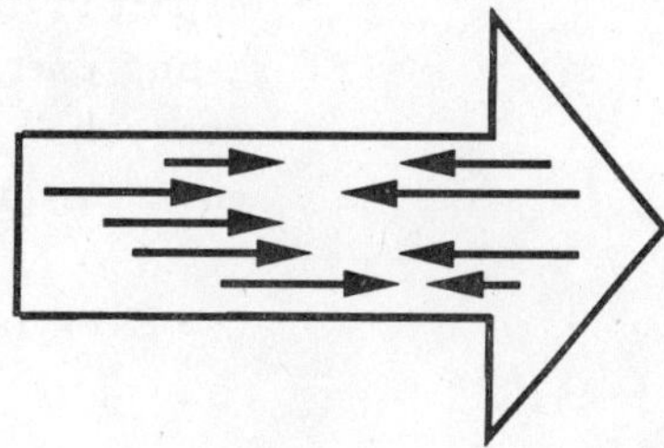

If we look at our model we see that the democratic process is typically made up of two different opinions. The group leader who gives the most convincing speech, or the one who has the best track record for getting things done, typically will win.

The advantages are:

- Decisions can be made fairly quickly.
- The majority opinion is used.

Disadvantages include:

- There are winners and losers.
- Those who lose may be counterproductive after they leave the room.
- All parties who vote on the subject should have equal knowledge.
- If the project fails the losers have the "I-told-you-so rights."
- Assumes equal knowledge of the subject.

The classic example of this is our two-party system of government. The one that does the best job of convincing the public to vote it into office must spend the next two or four years fighting the other side to keep its campaign promises.

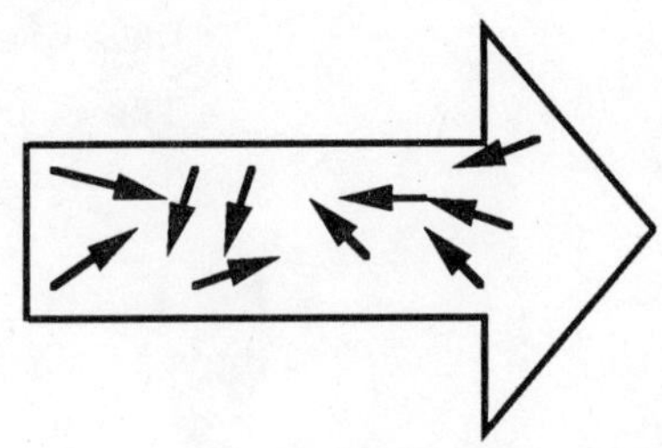

CONSENSUS STYLE

The consensus style is without a doubt the most difficult style of decision making to get used to, especially after operating under one of the other two styles for as long as most of us have. The consensus decision style recognizes that everyone has a different level of knowledge of the subject. This may range from someone who is an expert in the area to someone with no knowledge at all. The interesting part is that when a consensus decision process is working everyone's opinion will add something. Once mastered, the consensus style does have some distinct advantages. These are:

- Everybody wins.
- Unequal knowledge of the subject is welcomed.
- Everyone works toward the same goal.
- Time is spent productively.

Consensus has been reached when 70 percent of the group can buy into the decision 100 percent, and the remainder of the group can leave the room in support of the decision.

The consensus style of decision making is one of the strongest tools I have found for moving through the problem-solving process. Its strength lies in the fact that all of the possible issues and solutions are discussed and understood prior to moving forward. This gives the participants a real sense of ownership. Remember, not everyone understands the issue as well as you think you do. Even so, don't be afraid to listen to their opinions. They may help you understand the issues even better.

THE PROBLEM SPIDER

The Problem Spider is designed to assist you in placing a numerical value on an otherwise subjective issue. It will help you identify:

- The amount of *control* you exert.
- The amount of *resources* required.
- The anticipated *return on investment* (ROI).
- How *serious* the problem is.
- How much *time* will be needed *to solve* the problem.

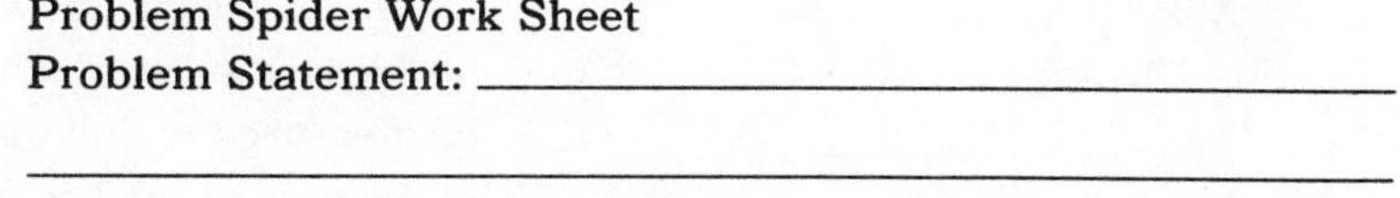
Problem Spider Work Sheet
Problem Statement: ______________________________

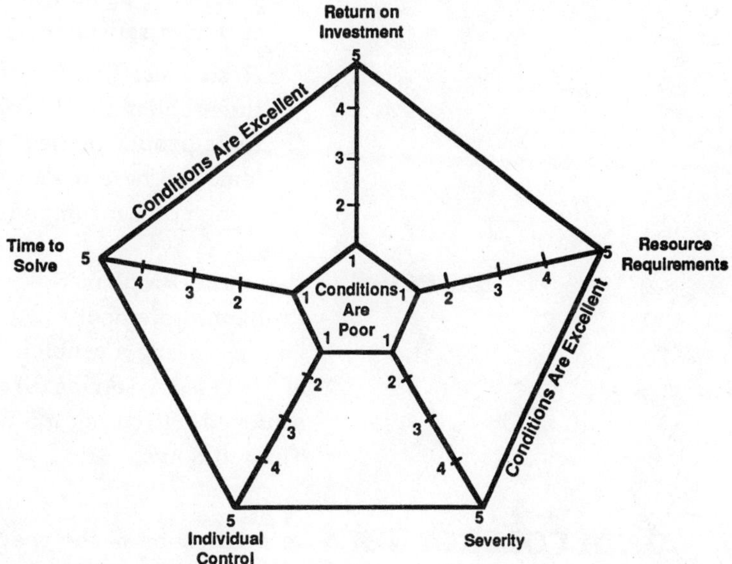

The Problem Spider

Rate each of the problems you select according to the Problem Spider. When you have assigned ratings for each item, add up the scores. The closer the total score is to 25 (the perfect score), the greater the possibility that you or your group can work effectively on the problem.

Let's look more closely at the five points of the diagram.

- *Control.* In Chapter 2 we defined five types of problems according to the extent of control you as an individual or group have in assisting toward the eventual outcome. In rating the existing conditions, 5 equals a high level of control over the situation.
- *Severity.* How serious is the problem? If it does not get fixed, what will the impact be? If it is a safety- or quality-related issue the need to fix the problem may be great. On the other hand, if it is a "nice-to-have" issue, the sense of urgency to fix the situation may not carry a high priority. Here a 5 would equal a very serious situation.
- *Time to Solve.* How much time will be involved to solve the problem? Look at everyone's time—not just yours. Here a 5 represents a problem that can be solved with a reasonable amount of time and effort.

- *Return on Investment.* What is the expected payback if the problem is solved? The payback of safety-related issues cannot be measured in dollars, so in those cases this does not apply. But, in the case of quality and cost projects, payback plays an important part. The question must be asked, "What is the payback?" Payback can be measured in both dollars and customer satisfaction. Here again a 5 represents a quick ROI or a high level of customer satisfaction.
- *Resources.* Simply put, these are the resources required to bring the problem to solution. Resources are defined as the amount of time, people, money, and equipment required to solve the problem. A 5 here means that the problem could be solved without tying up vast company resources.

EXERCISE

Using the Problem Spider, rate the problem you developed your Problem Statement for. Using this method of evaluation will assist you in picking a problem to work on that you can have some level of success in solving. Remember, a perfect score is 25. This is achieved by scoring a 5 in Severity, ROI, Control, Resources, and Time to Solve.

DATA COLLECTION TOOLS

In this section of the chapter we will discuss some of the tools that will assist you in the first phases of the problem-solving process. Here are some, but not all, of the techniques you can use to collect data as you begin the process.

OBSERVATION SHEETS

Observations sheets will:

- Identify the current method of performing the job.
- Offer a comparison between what you see and what others see.
- Allow you to compare the current method to design.

You can:

- Measure the difference between design and observed method.
- Identify design-sensitive activities.

The observation sheet is used to gather information about a machine, assembly, material, or procedure. The real strength of the observation sheet comes when it is used in the group format.

There are two forms of observations that are most helpful in analyzing manufacturing processes. They are visual observation and visual plus data.

VISUAL OBSERVATION

When performing visual observation in the workplace it is essential that the person doing the observing spend enough time on location to gather a complete picture of what is happening. To accomplish this there are a few courtesies that should be followed.

- Tell the person what you are doing and what you intend to do with the information you will collect. One of the worst things you can do is to cause people to think they are being spied on.
- Ask questions of the participants. There may be some things that may not be done during normal work cycles. To properly observe a job it is essential to understand everything the operator is expected to do.
- Write things down. Don't rely on your memory, write it down as you see it happen. Don't attempt to take extensive notes, use simple notes or shorthand.
- Spend the time necessary to fully understand what is happening. Nothing is more frustrating than dealing with a half a loaf of information. Poor decisions come from incomplete understanding.
- Take into account the model mix an operator will see while attempting to complete his job. In order to do this it may take several visits to the workplace.
- Take into account all of the tools and gages required to complete the job.
- If practical, share the results with the person or group being observed.

There are times when it is helpful to use *group observation,* that is, more than one person observe what is taking place. One reason for this is that your familiarity with a situation will sometimes blind you to what is really going on. People who work in an environment day in and day out get used to things and may develop personal prejudices about operations or processes.

Ask any attorney which he or she would prefer, one eyewitness to an event or a group of witnesses. I believe you will find that the defense would prefer the group, while the prosecutor would rather have the individual.

The method of processing group observations is simple. Use the same techniques you would use for brainstorming. Write down on a chart, pad, or chalkboard all of one individual's observations. Then have everyone else, in turn, add to the list, or identify the listed items they failed to observe. If you have an item that only one person has been able to identify, do not discount it. Go back and check; it may be the key.

VISUAL PLUS DATA

The second method of making observations is the same as the first, except that a gage reading, or some other type of quantifiable data, is collected. This method is used by floor inspectors, who make their periodic rounds of the manufacturing floor sampling parts and observing the manufacturing process. They would follow either a routine or a random cycle. Illustrated here is a sample of an auditor's data sheet taken in a department that makes steel spacers. What you see is the width of the spacers.

Part Name		Part #			Dept #
Operation #	Gage #	Characteristic	Gage Reading	Time	Comments

Making observations in this manner allows the observer to visualize any changes in the process. The hard data allow you to see immediately that there is some sort of problem. In a later chapter you will learn how to work with the information gathered in this chart.

TOOLS TO HELP YOU ANALYZE

CHECK SHEETS

Check sheets will identify the number of defects found by category. The information gathered can be used to develop Pareto charts (see below). In a typical check sheet possible defects are listed at the heads of the columns. An "X" is marked each time a defect of a particular type is detected.

SURVEYS

Surveys will identify:

- How customers feel about your product.
- How customers feel about your service.

Surveys will measure:

- Customer concern.
- Customer acceptance.
- Product readiness.

Surveys are questionnaires used to solicit the opinion of an individual or group with regard to things like housekeeping, quality, service, uptime, and customer satisfaction. They are an excellent tool in as much as they allow you to ask the question, and then follow up or probe for the reason behind the answer. Probing for clarification is helpful because it allows the individual to express his or her feelings. At times an individual's feelings will form the framework for understanding why he or she answered the question as they did. Additional data can then be collected and used in solving the problem.

Survey for Customer Satisfaction

1. **How do you feel about the products that are delivered to you from our department ?** ______________________
2. **Are they as good or better than those from other departments ?** ______________________
3. **What can we do to improve ?** ______________________

To conduct a survey,

- Decide what you want to know.
- Ask yourself why you want to know this.
- Ask yourself if you can get this information without doing a survey.
- Decide who you are going to survey.
- Determine the type of survey method you will use.
- Establish confidence limits for the survey.
- Develop a time line for the project.

You are now ready to develop the survey. To do so,

- Make a list of the resources (people and materials) necessary.
- Secure financial support for the survey.
- Draw a sample (choose people to be interviewed).
- Outline content areas and frame initial questions.
- Refine questions and design a workable format.
- Develop a first-draft questionnaire.

- Use pre-test findings to develop the final questionnaire.
- Teach interviewers how to gather and tabulate data.
- Establish a time line for the interview process.
- Conduct the interviews.
- Tabulate the data.
- Analyze the data.
- Determine a course of action—the action may be no action.

The personal interview

In conducting a survey, the personal interview is best used to secure information about complex topics that may require a great deal of explanation. The advantages of the personal interview are as follows:

- The interviewer can probe for additional information by observing the interviewee's reactions or body language.
- A high level of detail is obtained.
- More complex answers are given.
- The interviewer can use visual aids.
- Personal interaction often stimulates more cooperation and interest from respondents.

The disadvantages of the personal interview are as follows:

- It is the most costly in time, dollars, and data analysis, compared to other survey methods.
- The interviewer can bias questions, causing misleading answers.
- It requires a detailed data-collection process.
- The process is time-consuming.
- It is difficult to obtain standardized answers, due to the interviewer's influence.
- A high level of training is required for interviewers.

The mail survey

Mailing out questionnaires can broaden the information base of your investigation, or it can act to correlate the data from other forms of surveys. It is important that a detailed explanation of the purpose of the survey be enclosed with the mailing, along with a no-cost means of returning the information.

The advantages of the mail survey are as follows:

- It can provide a wide demographic view at a relatively low cost.
- It can be targeted at a specific audience or group.
- It avoids interviewer bias, resulting in honest answers.

- It can be done at the leisure of the individual, and may thus encourage him or her to take an interest in and respond to the questions.

The disadvantages of the mail survey are as follows:

- It can be time-consuming.
- Accurate mailing lists may not be available.
- Returns may not represent the feeling of the entire group surveyed. Individuals with a special interest in the survey subject may be more inclined to return the survey.
- Limited length of the questionnaire, which must be short enough that it does not intimidate the respondent.
- The inability of the developer to ensure that the question is understood and the answers properly recorded.
- It does not deal well with conceptual information.
- There is the question of who really completed the questionnaire.

The telephone survey

The telephone survey is best used when you have well-defined concepts, or a specific set of questions. The information should be limited and cannot be confidential.

The advantages of the telephone survey are as follows:

- It is fast.
- It is easy to control the target audience. Callbacks can be made if participants are busy.
- It has unlimited geographic reach.
- It has little bias due to closed-end questions.

The disadvantages of the telephone survey are as follows:

- It is limited to listed numbers only.
- It yields small amounts of information.
- It is difficult to judge the attitude of the respondent.

Asking questions

Within the three types of surveys are five ways of asking questions so that you can control the responses. This is important so that you can sort the data into meaningful groups during the analysis step of the process. The first is the *yes/no, or dichotomous, question:*

Did you like the overall appearance of the car? Yes ____ No ____

Did the performance of the vehicle meet your expectations? Yes ____ No ____

Was the car competitively priced? Yes ___ No ___

Would you buy this car? Yes ___ No ___

The advantages of asking questions in this manner are as follows:

- They provide specific answers.
- They provide a good lead-in for more-detailed questions.
- They are easy for the respondent to answer.
- They place little or no demand on the interviewer.

The disadvantages are as follows:

- They force the respondent to make a choice.
- They provide no explanation.
- They are difficult to word.

The second is the *"closed-end" question*. Examples of this type of question are:

What day of the week are you most likely to shop for a car?

Mon. ___ Tues. ___ Wed. ___ Thurs. ___ Fri. ___

What time of the day is your best time to shop for a car?

9 A.M. to 12 P.M. ___ 12 P.M. to 4 P.M. ___ 4 P.M. to 9 P.M. ___

The advantages of this type of question are as follows:

- They are short and easy to answer.
- They are quick to tabulate and analyze.
- Little or no demand is placed on the interviewer.

The disadvantages are as follows:

- It assumes all relevant answers are known.
- It can be difficult to word the questions.

The third type of question is the *multiple choice*, which offers the respondent a range of possible answers. Some examples might be:

Circle the answer that best describes the way you feel:

1. Would you say that your boss keeps you well-informed about the current state of the business? Well-informed Somewhat informed Not informed.

2. Are you satisfied with your current working conditions?
   Very satisfied
   Somewhat satisfied
   Neutral
   Somewhat dissatisfied
   Very dissatisfied

The advantages of using this type of question are as follows:

- The respondents are less likely to make an arbitrary choice.
- Findings are easy to tabulate and analyze.
- Constructed properly, it will list all possible alternatives.
- It is less demanding on the interviewer.
- It can be validated statistically by assigning a numerical value to each response.

The disadvantages are as follows:

- The questionnaire presupposes all relevant answers are known.
- Alternatives may have different meanings to the people being questioned.
- The order of choices or questions may bias answers.
- It may not present all alternatives and may therefore make it difficult for people to choose.

The fourth style of question is the one that asks the respondent to assign a *numerical rating* to each question. Examples are:
Rate on a scale of 1 to 5 how you feel about the following:

1. The paint job on this vehicle is 1—2—3—4—5
   (1 = excellent)
2. I have input into the design of my workplace.
   1—2—3—4—5—6—7
   Great Deal None

The advantages of this style of question are as follows:

- They can measure the intensity of the individual's feelings.
- Precise data can be collected if the intervals are equal.
- The data can be worked mathematically.

The disadvantages are as follows:

- The scale may not be clear to the respondent.

- The intervals may differ from the respondent's understanding of the situation.
- The respondent's perception may differ from the terms used.

The fifth and final type of question is the one where the respondent is asked to give his or her *"preference"* to a described situation. Examples are as follows:

To assist us in developing a list of items that are important to the customer who purchases a new car, please respond to the following as being either "very important" or "not very important" when you go out to purchase a new vehicle.

1. The dealer's showroom is well lit and the temperature is at a comfortable level. ____________
2. The car's finish is free of chips and runs. ____________
3. The car is perceived as having value. ____________

These are the advantages of putting questions in this form:

- Likes and dislikes are quick to surface.
- Feelings are clear when the relative magnitude is known.

These are the disadvantages:

- The real world can be overlooked.
- It may mentally fatigue respondents.

There is a second level that can be attached to most of these types of questions that allows those being polled to express themselves further. This is accomplished by asking the respondent to elaborate on one of the responses. A question asked in this manner would be as follows:

Would you buy this car? Yes ____ No ____ If no, please explain why not.

____

____

____

EXERCISE In this exercise you are to read the following paragraph and decide what types of surveys you are going to use. Then develop five questions for each of the questionnaires.

Your company has just released a complete redesign of an old product to the marketplace. You and your coworkers have been involved with this project right from the start, and are proud of your new baby. You and your group need two types of information to support your ongoing product development activities. First, you are interested in knowing how the buyers feel about the product they purchased and why they chose your brand. The second issue is *quality*. You are interested in knowing if there are any problems. You and your coworkers decide to develop a set of questionnaires to gather this information. Using the information learned in the section on questionnaires, first decide the type you will use, and then develop the questions for each.

Survey Type: ______________

Questions: ____

____

____

____

____

____

____

____

____

Survey Type: ______________

Questions: ____

____

____

____

____

____

____

____

____

PICTOGRAPHS

Pictographs will identify:

- Location of surface defects.
- Location of surface conditions.
- Location of processing defects, such as water and airleaks.

Pictographs will measure:

- Frequency of occurrence.
- Time of occurrence.

Pictographs are another tool to help you analyze data. They show the location and frequency of a product problem. You can make a pictograph by drawing a picture of the product and charting where and how often a problem occurs.

The shape of the product to be checked is shown on the pictograph. When a nonconformity is found, you can identify its size, shape, or location on the drawing of the product. This information can provide clues to the cause of a problem.

One drawback to pictographs is that a new sheet may be required each time a nonconformity occurs. You could end up with quite a stack of drawings to look at. It might be helpful to have a master drawing which compiles the information from the individual drawings.

In order to design and construct the most effective pictograph, you should have a clear understanding of what data are being collected and why. This understanding will help you design a pictograph to meet your needs.

Here are some "thought-starters," questions to ask yourself as you begin to develop your pictograph.

- Why am I doing this?
- What am I attempting to show?
- When will it be done (shift, time of day, etc.)?
- Where will the data collection take place?
- How will the data be collected?
- What units will the data be measured in?
- Who will do the data collection?
- How will the data be used?

When deciding what material to include, remember that the data may not be analyzed right away, or may be analyzed by someone else. This makes it important to include all of the details that will allow someone else to understand and use the data.

The primary purpose of a pictograph is to provide the user with a visual means of identifying problem areas. Pictographs are normally used to analyze surface finish of metal stampings, paint quality, water leaks, and surface flatness. To assist you in better understanding pictographs, let's develop two samples, one plain and one using a frequency chart.

The first example is one that is typically used in identifying the surface quality of sheet metal stampings. The first step is to outline the stamping on a graph paper. Here are some suggestions in developing pictographs for sheet metal parts.

- Select graph paper with a large-enough grid.
- Indicate the grid size (for example, 100 mm × 100 mm).
- Select a scale that will allow you to get the part to be drawn on an 8.5″ × 11″ sheet of graph paper.
- Develop the view of the part that best represents the problem area.
- Identify the problem areas on the picture, along with the comments that best describe the problem.

Of the two methods of using a pictograph, use the one below when periodic checks of a part are to be made. You might check one sample per day or shift, looking for a particular discrepancy. This method can also be used by skilled employees. The example demonstrates a typical pictograph to determine surface discrepancies of a sheet metal stamping. Here you would attempt to show the following:

- Location of defect(s)
- Relative severity of defect.
- Description of defect.

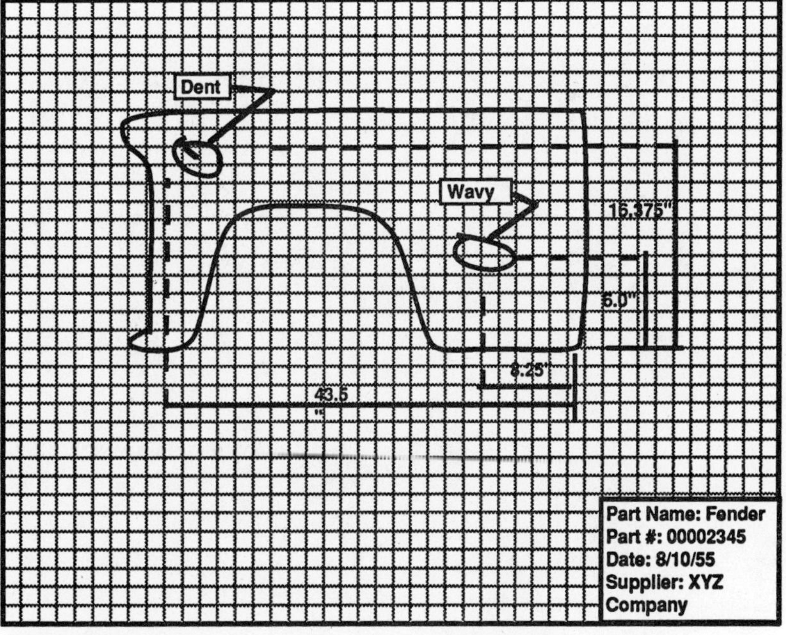

Pictograph to Determine Surface Discrepancies

Pictograph with frequency chart

Our next example demonstrates the second method used with pictographs. In it we attempt to determine the flatness of a machined surface, looking for variation across the face of the part. Here we will use more than one sample looking for variation from part to part also. This type of pictograph is helpful in analyzing machine performance prior to making any adjustments.

In this example we have a cast iron part that is being milled from a finished surface. Our inspection department has informed us that the machined surfaces are not parallel, that there are some areas that are lower than others.

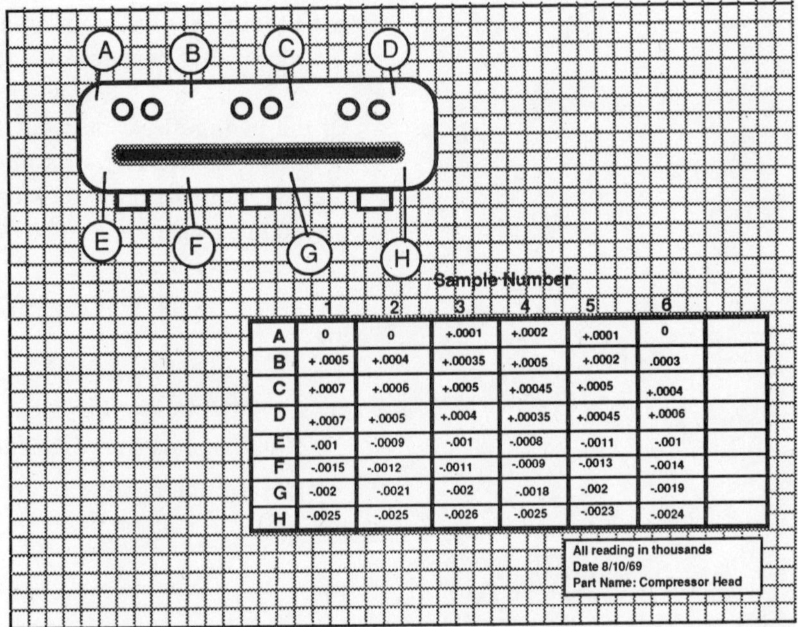

	1	2	3	4	5	6	
A	0	0	+.0001	+.0002	+.0001	0	
B	+ .0005	+.0004	+.00035	+.0005	+.0002	.0003	
C	+.0007	+.0006	+.0005	+.00045	+.0005	+.0004	
D	+.0007	+.0005	+.0004	+.00035	+.00045	+.0006	
E	-.001	-.0009	-.001	-.0008	-.0011	-.001	
F	-.0015	-.0012	-.0011	-.0009	-.0013	-.0014	
G	-.002	-.0021	-.002	-.0018	-.002	-.0019	
H	-.0025	-.0025	-.0026	-.0025	-.0023	-.0024	

All reading in thousands
Date 8/10/69
Part Name: Compressor Head

Pictograph to Check for Parallelism and Flatness

Our chart shows that points A through D are not parallel to points on the opposite side of the machined surface. In this case we would be required to position the locators on the side represented by E through H.

Chapter 4

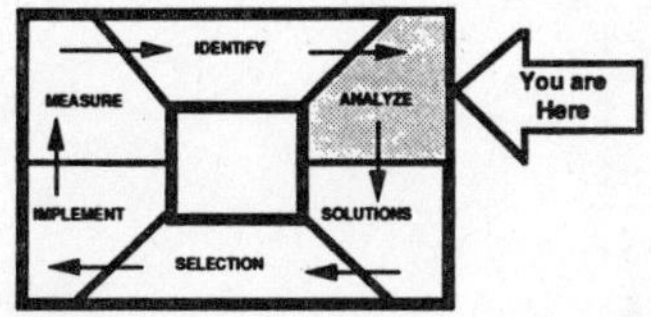

ANALYZING THE PROBLEM

Once you have identified or selected a problem to work on, the next task you are faced with is to find out everything about it. This means working out a plan to research and discover facts relevant to the problem you have identified.

Remember that the nature of the issue will often determine how it is to be analyzed. Technical, interpersonal, contractual, and policy issues are some of the types of issues you may face. In each case the analysis would be handled differently, using different sources, techniques, and data. To understand how you might develop your plan of attack, take a look at the following steps:

ESTIMATING POSSIBLE CAUSE

First, we need to know what type of data to collect in order to get an accurate and complete understanding of the problem. Therefore, the first step is to identify what you think *may* be causing the problem. Once you do this you will have a good idea of the scope of the fact finding that must be carried out. One of the best tools in the fact-finding process is the fishbone, or cause-and-effect diagram (see page 61).

IDENTIFYING THE KEY INGREDIENTS

As we saw in Chapter 2, the process of problem solving will include one or more of the following ingredients: Man, Machine, Method, Measurement, and Environment. These are the main contributors to the manufacturing process. Once we understand them—and how each contributes to the process—we can begin our research. Remember from Chapter 2 that if the process is varying from the accepted performance standard, it should be analyzed to determine the root cause of the problem.

As pictured here, the following six ingredients are mixed together, in the correct amounts, to produce a salable product.

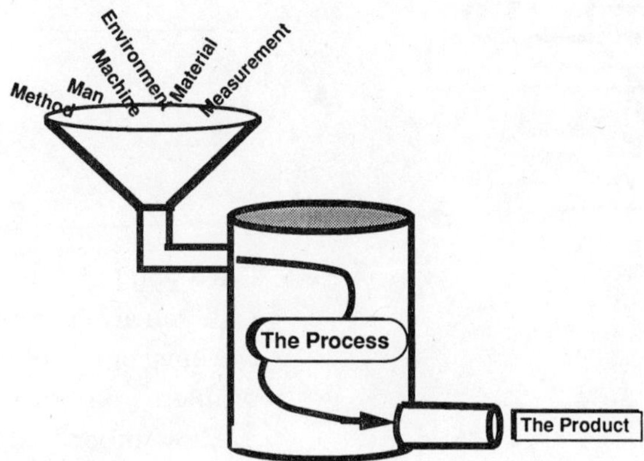

- Man. The operator, inspector, engineers, supervisors, and managers all influence the expected results. The key in dealing in this arena is to create an environment of cooperation and understanding, not one of blame. This is a prime responsibility of management.
- Machine. These can be as simple as a hammer or as complex as a computer-controlled, multi-station machine which takes a rough casting and turns it into a finished product. The definition of machine commonly includes the tooling, fixtures, cutting fluids, and oils that assist the machine.
- Methods. The method is the direction, procedures, or sequence a person should follow in order to accomplish the task. These can come in the form of written job instruction, pictures, or flow diagrams.
- Material. Here we include any of the materials that go into making the product. They might include castings, forgings, stampings, gaskets, sealants, or fasteners, to name a few.
- Measurement. This would include everything from the actual measurement of the product for dimensional items to daily output to determine the performance standard.
- Environment. The environment, as I prefer to call it, breaks down into areas of the physical environment such as temperature, humidity, lighting, and air quality.

DETERMINING THE WHATS AND THE WHYS

At this step of the problem-solving process I have found it helpful to develop what I call a "What-and-Why" chart, not to be confused with the "Five Whys" method of root cause analysis below. The "What-and-Why" chart is one method I use to jump-start my thought processes, which follow the axiom laid out in Murphy's law, "If anything can go wrong it will." To develop your chart, follow three simple steps:

- State the problem as you know it.
- List all the things that could possibly have caused the stated problem.
- Explain what effect each has on the stated problem.

A "What-and-Why" chart looks very similar to a family tree. We are still looking for probable cause, with no attempt to carry it any further than that.

FISHBONE, OR CAUSE-AND-EFFECT DIAGRAM

One of the best tools to use when estimating possible cause is the Fishbone, or Cause-and-Effect diagram. This tool can be used for both the unexpected problem and the selected problem, as discussed in Chapter 3. In the unexpected problem, the diagram clarifies what may be the cause(s) of the discrepancy between the as-is situation and the existing goal. In the selected problem, the diagram clarifies the factors that will help you move toward your new goal.

The fishbone diagram supplies information about the problem in two ways. First, it provides a visual means of tracing a problem to its most likely cause. This is one of the fishbone's strongest assets. The ability to first collect and then visually see possible cause is a real source of motivation for the individual or the group. Second, the diagram shows how the causes relate to the problem and to each other. Being able to visualize the possible causes, you can quickly begin to relate where a problem in one area may have its roots in another.

Notice that the basic structure looks like the skeleton of a fish. The problem is stated at the head of the fish. Major possible causes are listed on the ribs, and other contributing factors can be included on the bones of the fish.

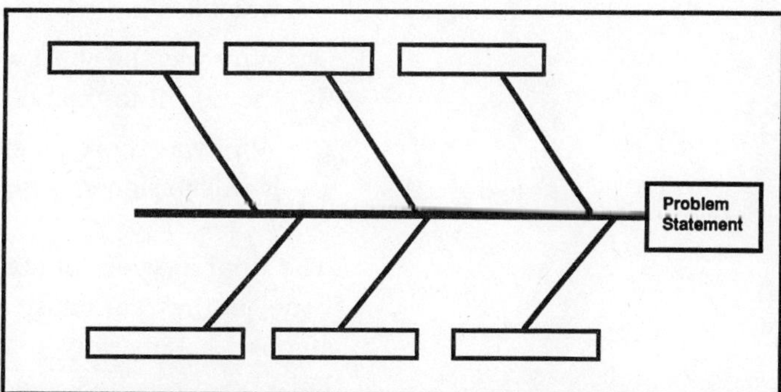

The Fishbone Diagram (A)

Most problems are solved more effectively by using the combined abilities of members of work groups or teams. The Fishbone is an excellent tool to use because it allows you or the group to record your ideas in an organized manner. It also allows you to visualize the relationship of the possible cause or causes to the problem itself. To construct a fishbone diagram,

- Identify the problem.
- Identify the categories of causes.
- Generate a list of all causes.
- Evaluate the list of causes.

Defining the problem: The "five whys"

Too often a problem is not fully solved, or goes away for a while and then comes back. In these cases we have been working on a symptom and not on the real problem. The preferred method for determining the root cause of a problem is a simple one: ask "Why" at least five times. For example,

- Why do we do it this way?
- Why did things turn out this way?
- Why shouldn't we try it this way?

Suppose that a machine's motor has stopped. This is the third time we have replaced it, and we are about to put on the fourth motor in as many days. Should we find out why it has failed? Let's use the "Five Whys" rule to find out why it stopped.

- Why did the motor stop? The fuse was blown because of an overload.
- Why did it get overloaded? Because there was not enough lubrication on the shaft.
- Why was there not enough oil? Because the lube pump was not pumping at full volume.
- Why was the pump's output low? Because the pump shaft was worn down.
- Why was the shaft worn down? Because there was no strainer in the oil fill tank and metal shavings got mixed in with the oil.
- Why was there no strainer in the fill neck of the tank? Because it was designed without one.

The final answer, which would be entered into the head of the fishbone, is the real cause behind all of the other "Whys." If we had stopped asking why before the last one, the real cause would not have been reached. We would spend our time attempting to solve a symptom and not the problem.

Example

Suppose the result of an unsolved problem is oil on the floor. We would begin the problem-solving exercise by asking

- Why is there oil on the floor? The machine is leaking.
- Why is the machine leaking? The fitting on the machine comes loose.
- Why does the fitting come loose? There is a vibration in the hydraulic line.
- Why is there a vibration in the hydraulic line? Because the pump is putting out too much pressure.
- Why is the pump putting out too much pressure? Because it is improperly adjusted.

If we could not develop this any further, then the head of our fishbone, the problem statement, would read "Improper Adjustment."

Identifying the categories of cause

Next, the categories of cause of the problem (or factors that will help you move toward your new goal in a selected problem situation) are entered onto the ribs of the fish. As stated earlier, these are usually "Man," "Method," "Machine," "Material," "Measurement," and "Environment." Whether you are solving the problem individually or in a group, as you think of possible causes categorize and write them down at the appropriate rib of the fishbone diagram.

Any or all six categories represent a good starting point for developing your problem-solving process. Feel free to add categories as you determine they are needed.

These categories will help you to organize all of the possible causes of the problem, and are the major elements of the fishbone. They are shown here.

Finally, write a "Causal Analysis of Problems" and evaluate your results.

EXERCISE

What seems to be the major cause or causes of the problem? Write this down in the space provided; it will help you in the next phases of the process.

Causal Analysis: ____

____

____

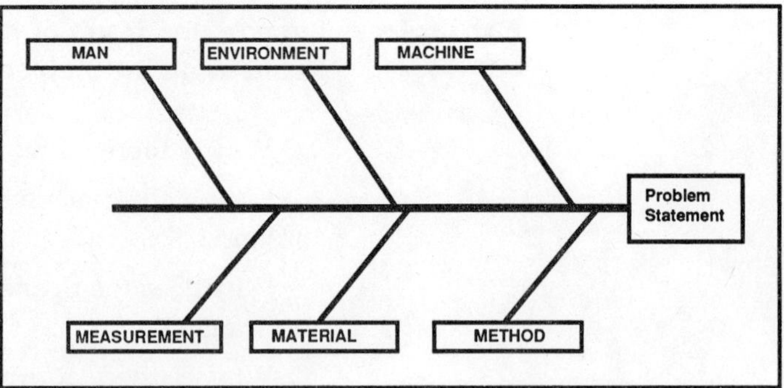

The Fishbone Diagram (B)

Generating and evaluating a list of all causes

The next step in constructing a fishbone diagram is to generate and then evaluate a complete list of all possible causes of the problem. List as many possible causes of the problem that you or your team can think of. The best technique for this is brainstorming (see Chapter 3). Another suggestion is to develop a What-and-Why chart.

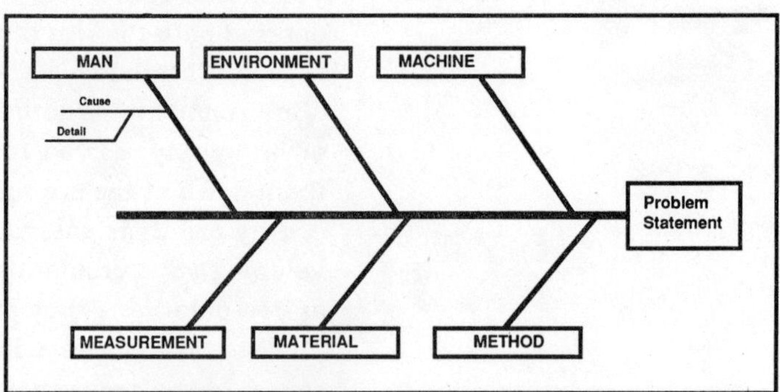

The Fishbone Diagram (C)

Next, discuss the list of possible causes. Questions about the ideas should be explained and similar ideas combined. Here, as with the head of the fish, "Why" should be asked as many times as necessary to eliminate listed causes as possible problems.

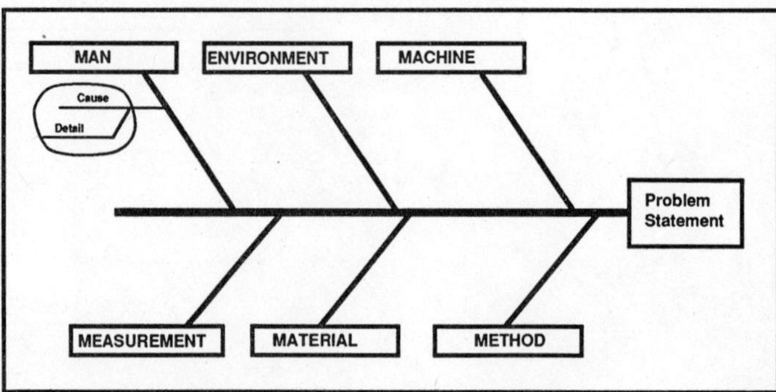

The Fishbone Diagram (D)

Ideas that don't belong on the diagram should be removed. The goal of this step is to improve the diagram. This evaluation process is directed only at the ideas. Remember, each of the items identified represents a possible cause that must be researched. No idea(s) should be considered dumb or far-fetched without investigation. Only after investigation can any of the "thought-starters" be removed from the diagram.

EXERCISE Using the problem you have identified, use a separate sheet of paper to develop a fishbone diagram.

DEVELOP A RESEARCH PLAN

You are now ready to develop a research plan or, as some might call it, a plan of attack. Working with your problem statement, determine what your information needs are and the techniques you will use to gain that information. Next, write down a step-by-step plan of how you intend to go about getting it.

Your problem is that the parts you are machining in one part of the process seem to be changing size as they progress through the process. The parts are thin-wall cylinders which must be held to a very close tolerance. The first step is to establish the rules of the investigation process. I have included some as "thought-starters" for the problem stated above. There may be more. See if you can think what they are?

- All tests should be developed by following the same parts through the steps in the process.
- All test parts must be numbered to assist in identifying them.
- All sample sizes will be 50 pieces.

Any variance from these rules must be noted on the information sheets.

Once the rules have been established, the next step is to develop the process by which you will go about collecting the information required. Some sample statements from a research plan for this problem might look like this:

- Look at the size and out-of-round condition as the part leaves the rough-turning operation.
- Number 50 parts prior to the rough-turning operation.
- Mark a line on the part flange.
- Change and adjust tools or the machine.
- Scribe line on the top face of the chuck.
- Locate all parts on the chuck so that the lines match.
- Run parts without interruption.
- Check the diameter of all of the parts in the following manner: at the scribed line, and then at 60 degree intervals. Record the

results. As part of this you must also decide what form you want your data in. There are many techniques for acquiring data.

EXERCISE

Using the problem you identified, develop a research plan. Remember to identify your information needs, how you will collect that information, and the time required to complete each task. It is helpful to write down what you expect to prove by collecting each parcel of data.

IDENTIFY YOUR DATA REQUIREMENTS

As part of your research plan you should be developing what you feel your data requirements will be and what form you want them in. It is at this point that you should be thinking about any special forms you should have to make the data collection easier and understandable.

1 2 3

Date: ____________

Describe method:

Sketch

Part #	1	2	3	Comments

To accomplish this you should develop a list of all the information you will require in order to come to a complete understanding of the problem. Ask the basic questions "What," "Where," "When," and "How" to help you know what you must research.

For example, in our research plan we identified a need to measure our cylinders in three places. To keep that information in an orderly manner you might want to develop a simple data acquisition sheet like the one on page 66. The company you are working for may already have sheets like this available.

Remember that it may be helpful to compare the situation you have with your problem to the situation of other departments or sections in the plant. Do not limit the sources or kinds of information to your own area.

HANDS-ON EXPERIENCE

Hands-on experience is invaluable in understanding problems. Typically, problems today are dealt with by long distance. Under normal conditions, if a problem arises in a manufacturing situation the product and process engineers start with the premise that everything they have done up to this point is O.K. My personal experiences in this area have been profound:

As part of an early training program in preparation for a career in manufacturing I was assigned to work as a production operator in every machining and assembly department in the plant. The year I spent working in the factory provided me with a great deal of insight in two areas. The first was that the real experts are those who run the job every day, and that good people can make a bad process work. Until recently the voices of these experts went unheard when it came to solving their problems in their work area. For a better understanding of a problem, go to the area and perform the task. The experience will enhance your ability to understand the problem. Remember what Aristotle said, "If you want to know what is going on in the city, spend some time at the grindstone." This only reinforces the fact that the information required to solve problems cannot be found in the office.

This is particularly true of technical or process problems involving difficulties with machinery, or written instructions, or filling out documents. From this experience you can then determine what methods of data collection could be used.

PAPER RESEARCH

Many problems can be understood only by understanding policies, rules, and procedures which influence what happens. You will need to collect copies of all the relevant documents. It is helpful at times to write down exactly what you think must be done to achieve the desired results.

Typically, a paper of this type would start with your goal statement (see Chapter 3). You will then write down what you feel is necessary to achieve the determined goal. Simply write it down and use it as a working document to follow during your problem-solving process.

DATA COLLECTION

Collect the data you have identified as necessary to assist you in better understanding the problem. Remember, as you begin to collect data you may find that you need additional information. At this point it is wise to revise the list of information to be collected so that nothing is lost or forgotten. Listed below are some of the tools and what they can accomplish. Detailed descriptions of how to use each of these are found later on in this chapter.

Pareto analysis

Factors in a problem are divided into categories and shown on a graph in rank order, larger to smaller, from left to right. The data may be shown in absolute numbers or in percentages. The 80:20 rule is an example of Pareto analysis. Pareto analysis will often show the major cause of a problem.

- Pareto diagrams will identify your problems in rank order.
- Pareto diagrams will measure your successes in your efforts to solve problems.

Histograms

Histograms, or bar charts, show the distribution of some characteristics of the problem. The main advantage of histograms and other charts of this type is the visual image they provide the user. This display allows the user to see how the data that has been collected relate. The visual effect makes it a powerful tool.

Histograms will identify:

- Ability of current process.
- Ability after improvement.
- If the process is centered.
- If the process is making good parts.

Histograms will measure:

- Process capability.
- If correction must be made.
- Operator sensitivity.
- Vendor capability.

and will evaluate any problem-solving efforts.

Graphs

Graphs show the distribution or changes in some factor on two axes, such as time and incidence.

Flowcharts

Flowcharts are a tool used to show the flow of materials, work content of a job, or any other process where multiple steps are involved. There are several different types of flowcharts, which we will address later on in this chapter. They are process, branching, line, and layout.

Flowcharts will identify

- current processes
- possible wasted activities
- interferences in planning
- excessive storage locations

EVALUATION OF THE DATA

When you have collected and displayed the data you can now begin the evaluation process.

A note of caution. The six-step approach to problem solving is a process and must be carried out in a sequence. Most people are not used to following a consistent process when they solve problems, which is one of the reasons they get into difficulties. So when people first start using the process, they often find it uncomfortable and time-consuming. The temptation is to jump or short-circuit steps in order to move quickly. DO NOT DO THIS. After a while, the process will come much more naturally to you and it will come faster—without losing the benefits of the discipline approach.

Remember: Document
Document
Document

TOOLS TO HELP YOU ANALYZE DATA

We will give you examples and uses of some of the more common ones.

PROCESS FLOWCHARTS

There are many different kinds of flowcharts that can be used to analyze problems in the manufacturing process. In order to properly problem-solve any manufacturing process, we must first understand the process itself, that is, how the process is organized. Proper process and workstation organization is essential to manufacturing a high-quality part.

Flowcharts can be created through an individual or team effort. If you are working in a team or group, have the facilitator or leader write down on a chart pad the steps in the process as they are identified. To check to make sure no steps have been missed, it is best to walk through the process using the flowchart you have developed. Missing, incomplete, or confusing steps should be spotted and clarified during this review process.

The process flowchart is a broad-form, graphic representation of what work is being performed on the product and in what sequence.

It looks at the product and the manufacturing functions that must be completed to produce it. Typically, this type of flowchart is used to analyze:

- Product movement.
- People movement.
- Paper movement.

To help you develop a flowchart that may be easily understood and immediately used by everyone, common symbols have been agreed on. Some symbols and their interpretations are shown here.

Symbols	Name	Description
O	Operation	This symbol is used when there is work being performed on the product. An example might be machining, assembly, disassembly, etc.
T	Transportation	This symbol is used when an object is moved from one place to another.
Insp.	Inspection	This symbol is used when an object is checked for either quantity or quality.
D	Planned Delay	This symbol is used when an object is is retained in storage awaiting an activity. No authorization is required to move the object.
S	Storage	This symbol is used when the material is is placed in storage and is protected against unauthorized removal or movement.

These symbols may be used to develop both simple, or straight-line flowcharts and complex, or branching flowcharts. Here is an example of a simple, or basic, straight-line flowchart showing a straight manufacturing process.

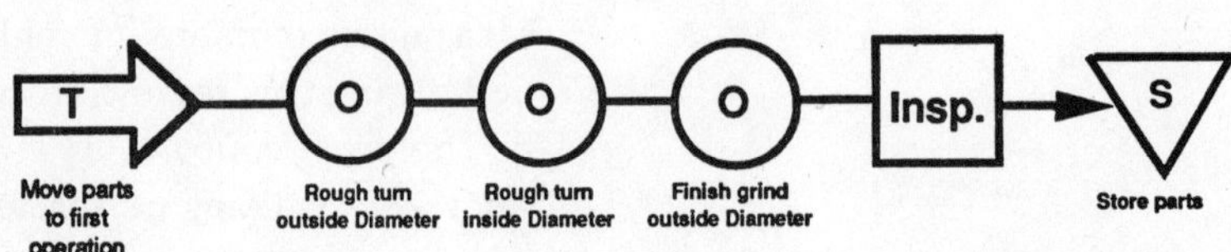

This is an example of a multi-line flowchart representing two processes that eventually merge into one.

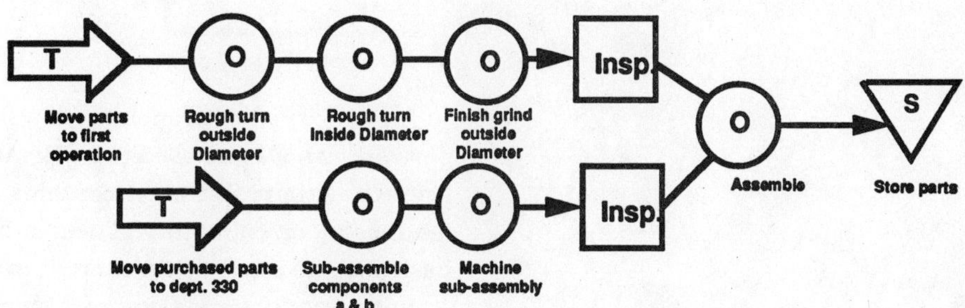

Flowcharts of this type can be used to answer some of the following questions:

- Can the operation be eliminated?
- Can the operation be combined with another operation?
- Can or should the sequence be changed?
- Can the operation be simplified?
- Can some movement be eliminated?
- Can a delay or storage area be eliminated?
- Can this whole step be eliminated or redesigned?

Branching flowcharts

The complex, or branching flowcharts are made by joining together two or more straight-line charts. This type may be used to study multiple processes that must come together to complete a process or product. An example of this might be individual parts coming together for a subassembly, or subassemblies coming together at final assembly. Typically, information included in the chart(s) might be quantity, distance moved, type of work done, and equipment used. Work times may also be included. Here are some additional symbols, to be used in branching flowcharts.

Symbols	Description
Entry or Exit Point	This symbol is used to enter or exit the flowchart.
Decision Box	This symbol is used to identify the need for a decision to be made.

Instruction Box	**This symbol is used to provide instructions to the user.**

Another type of branching flowchart used to track the flow of paperwork can also be used to track manufacturing processes. It differs from the others in that it contains one or more decision node(s) or feedback loop capability. The symbols used in this type of chart are basically the same as those used in regular branching charts.

In the paperwork flowchart shown here we are tracking a work order through the system. You can see what happens if the paperwork is properly filled out and is accepted as a viable project. You can also see what happens if the reverse is true.

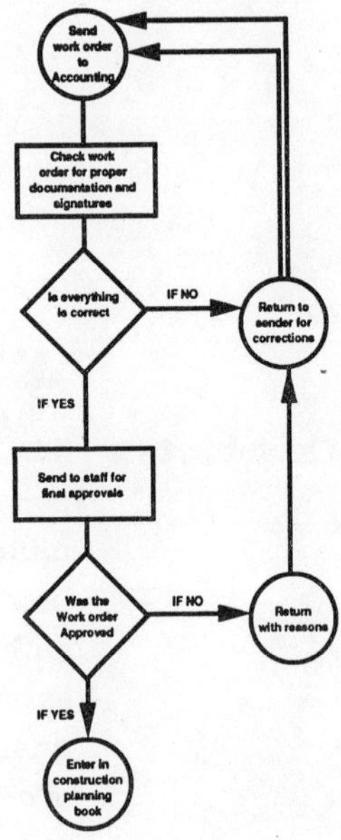

In summary, a flowchart is a valuable tool that can be used in the early stages of problem identification and analysis. By analyzing the steps in the flowchart, the individual or team can come to a better understanding of what is currently going on in the manufacturing process. You will be able to spot possible causes and potential solutions to the problem you are attempting to solve.

WORKSTATION DESIGN

Workstation design will identify:

- Current method of operation.
- Tools used in process.
- Path of operator.

- Time to complete.
- Parts used and their placement.

Workstation design can measure:

- Improvements made to process.

Workstation design work sheets are used to take the process flow to the operator level. The real value of this type of analysis can best be seen when quality problems and situations involving continuous improvement are involved. To effectively use this method of analysis, a separate sheet must be done for each operator working in an area. When completed, the individual sheets can be overlaid. The purpose of this is to look for interferences caused by physical intrusion, tool usage, fixture placement, and so on.

Remember, the purpose of the workstation design is to identify all of the elements that make up the job as either operations, storage, or inspection.

- *Operations* is defined as performing work directly on the product.
- *Storage* is defined as putting new material, or material you have subassembled, into storage racks of some kind.
- *Inspection* is defined as checking the product to ensure that your work and the work of others has been performed correctly.

By looking at all parts of an operation, you can determine what is required to accomplish the whole task. This works for an individual or an entire group working in the same area. To start the development of your workstation design, you must first identify all of the tasks necessary to complete one work cycle.

On the work sheet we should see the following details called for:
Customary items:

- Step number
- A brief description of the task
- The time required to complete the work
- The walk time involved
- Cumulative time for the entire operation
- Tooling

Optional items:

- Part numbers
- Actual steps required

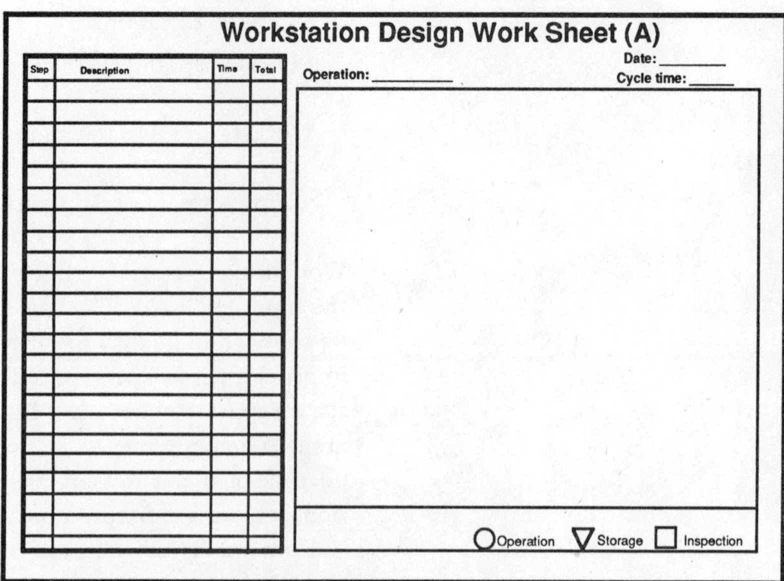

Workstation Design Work Sheet (A)

Date: ________

Operation: ________

Cycle time: ______

Step	Description	Time	Total

Workstation Design Work Sheet (A)

Having identified the tasks required to perform the entire work cycle, make a scale drawing of your workstation:

- Step 1. Accurately identify the size and location of everything in the workplace, including such things as storage racks, worktables, tools, tool rails, mechanical assist devices, and so on.
- Step 2. Draw the actual layout.

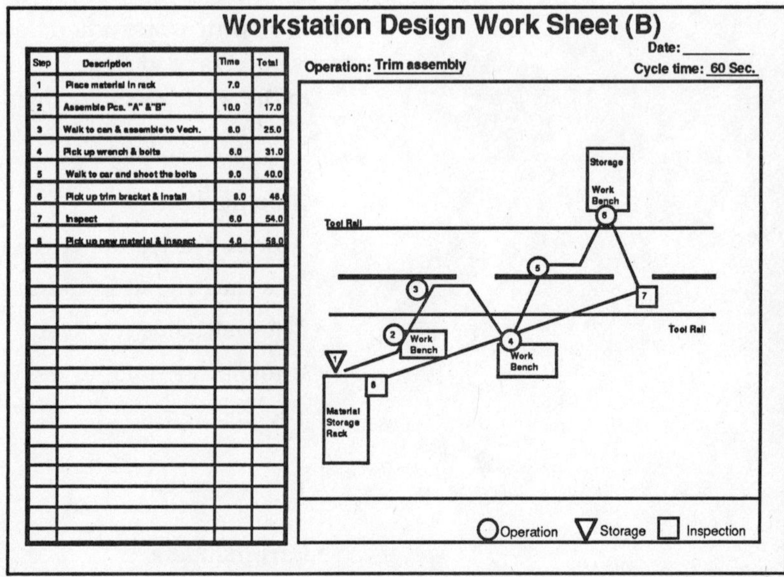

Workstation Design Work Sheet (B)

Date: ________

Operation: Trim assembly

Cycle time: 60 Sec.

Step	Description	Time	Total
1	Place material in rack	7.0	
2	Assemble Pcs. "A" &"B"	10.0	17.0
3	Walk to can & assemble to Vech.	8.0	25.0
4	Pick up wrench & bolts	6.0	31.0
5	Walk to car and shoot the bolts	9.0	40.0
6	Pick up trim bracket & install	8.0	48.(
7	Inspect	6.0	54.0
8	Pick up new material & inspect	4.0	58.0

Workstation Design Work Sheet (B)

- Step 3. Trace your path through the entire work cycle, using the symbols for operations, storage, and inspection previously described.

Workstation design layouts or work sheets provide several valuable services:

- They provide a visual means of looking at what you actually do to perform your job, as well as the time and tools required. This information is necessary in the problem-solving process.
- They provide an excellent tool to educate new operators. These work sheets have all of the information necessary to complete the job, including time, tools, and the path required.
- They provide a means of describing the standardized process for your particular operation.
- They provide an accurate description of each operation in the factory that could be used to duplicate the process if business improves.

Workstation design is a necessary tool in the continuous improvement and synchronous manufacturing processes.

WORK-AND-WAIT ANALYSIS

Work-and-wait analysis will identify:

- The amount of time a part spends in each segment of the operation.
- Where your inventory is.
- Where improvements can be made.
- Where your current operation is, in relation to the ideal.

Work-and-wait analysis will measure:

- Any improvements you make.

The work-and-wait analysis process is a hybrid of the man/machine analysis process. It has been designed around a very simple principle, and that is the elimination of all wasted activity in any single operation. Waste, in this case, is defined as time in any operation during which there is no added-value activity being performed.

List all steps

To eliminate time spent waiting, first identify *all* of the steps required to complete the operation. The operation we are using here as an example is one required to manufacture water pumps. This work-and-wait analysis process can also be used to analyze service activities, including office functions.

Step#	*Description*
1	Rough turn inside pump cavity & rough bore shaft hole.
2	Stack on conveyor four high using wooden dividers.
3	Load dial machines to drill and tap cover & plug holes.
4	Stack on conveyor four high using dividers.
5	Finish bore shaft hole.
6	Finish bore and face impeller cavity.
7	Wash.
8	Stack on conveyor prior to assembly.
9	Assemble and stack in shipping baskets.

Determine the time

We are now ready to identify the amount of time a part or container spends at each step of the operation, for example, time spent in storage prior to the part being loaded into the operation. Where practical, all steps should be listed separately so that each can be exposed and eventually worked on. To accomplish this we take the above list of operations in the water pump manufacturing process and add the times spent.

Step #	*Description*	*Time*
1	Rough turn inside pump cavity & rough bore shaft hole.	1.5 hours
2	Stack on conveyor four high using wooden dividers.	1.0 hours
3	Load dial machines to drill and tap cover & plug holes.	1.33 hours
4	Stack on conveyor four high using dividers.	1.0 hours
5	Finish bore shaft hole.	.66 hours
6	Finish bore and face impeller cavity.	.75 hours
7	Wash.	.75 hours
8	Stack on conveyor prior to assembly.	1.0 hours
9	Assemble and stack in shipping baskets.	.50 hours
	Total	7.54 hours

The difference between the total 7.5 hours and 8 hours represents the employees' lunch break.

Graph the process

Having listed all steps and determined the time spent on each, you can now develop the base chart:

- Step 1. Draw the work-and-wait frame. Scale is important on the vertical or Y axis. It should be developed in increments that will allow you to accurately chart your times.

Work-and-Wait Chart (A)

- Step 2. Add the work-and-wait columns on the vertical or X axis.

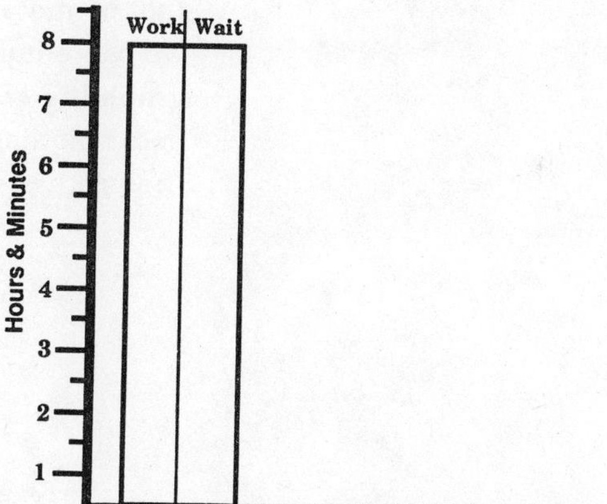

Work-and-Wait Chart (B)

- Step 3. Begin plotting your activities as shown, putting the steps in sequential order as shown. Try to be as accurate as possible when plotting your time intervals.

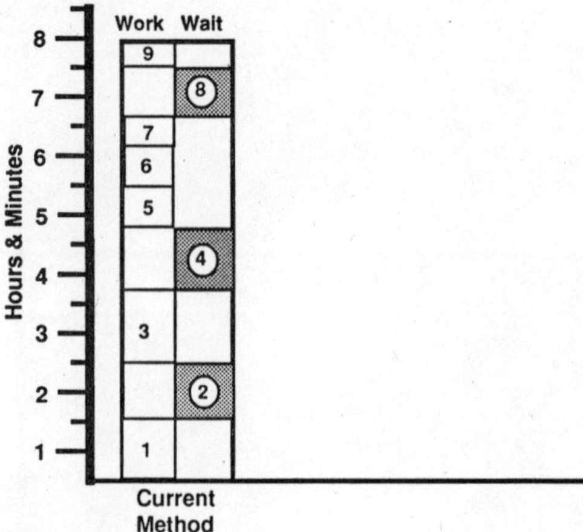

Work-and-Wait Chart (C)

Once you have completed plotting your activities, spend some time analyzing what can be done to eliminate the time required for steps that add no value to the product or service. Once you have analyzed the process, determine if it is possible to shorten or eliminate any of the steps on the wait side of the bar.

- Step 4. As an example of this, let's say that we have determined that by moving the machines that perform steps 1 and 3 together we can eliminate the storage between the two operations. Let's graph the changes and look at what this would do to our work-and-wait diagram. This step should be done each time you revise the process or service.

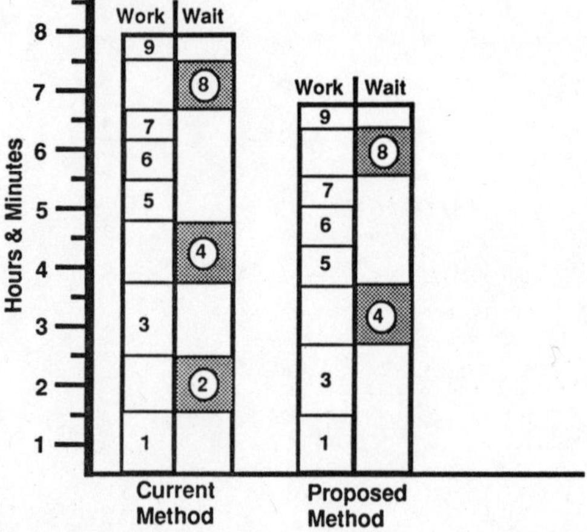

Work-and-Wait Chart (D)

- Step 5. The last step in the work-and-wait analysis is to determine what the ideal process or service flow ought to look like. This should be determined by estimating the shortest possible time all of the value-added activities could be performed in, and the total elimination of all of the wait time. Look at the last graph to see what the ideal time for our example would be. Remember, the objective is always to work toward achieving the ideal process.

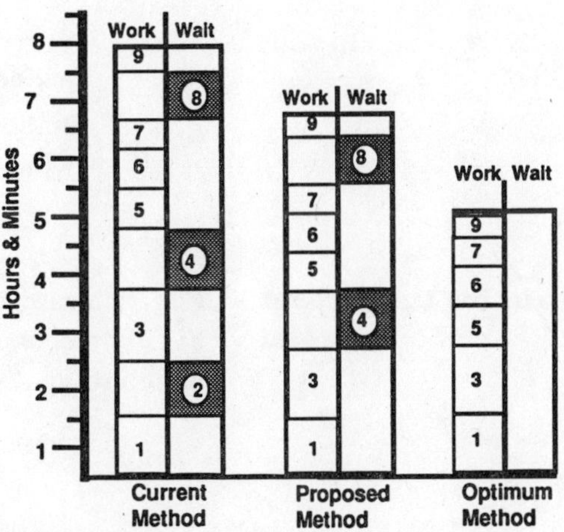

Work-and-Wait Chart (E)

PARETO DIAGRAMS

With many problem-solving efforts it is difficult to decide where to start. There may be a large number of problems or causes. You or your team must sort through to select the one that is most important.

The Pareto diagram is a bar chart that ranks items under investigation in descending order, based on their frequency of occurrence or cost. The idea is to establish which problems are occurring most frequently, or are costing you the most in lost production or dollars.

There are three major uses of Pareto diagrams. They help

- Identify where to begin the problem-solving process.
- Determine the relative seriousness of the problems or causes of problems.
- Show the results of your improvement effort.

Constructing Pareto diagrams

The first step in constructing a Pareto chart is to identify which problems or causes you want to track. You can do this by using some of the other techniques in this handbook such as observation, brainstorming, fishbone diagrams, histograms, and so forth. Other sources of information might be scrap or rework reports or machine downtime records.

The next step is to collect data on the number of times, or frequency, a problem occurs. If you are monitoring a problem you might like to know how often the problem occurs by shift, day, week, or month.

Start by gathering all of the information relative to the area being studied. A sample data sheet might look like this:

Category	*Frequency*	*Percent of Total*
Other	440 pcs.	9.7
Broken tap	1200 pcs.	26.5
No tap	600 pcs.	13.2
Drilled deep	950 pcs.	21.0
Shallow tap	800 pcs.	17.6
Drilled shallow	545 pcs.	12.0
Total Defects	4535 pcs.	100.0

Calculating the percent of total

For each category divide the frequency of defects by the total number of defects. In our sample the percent of holes drilled shallow can be found by dividing 545 by 4535.

$$545/4535 = 12.0\%$$

Arranging the information

The next step would be to arrange the information in descending order. In our example, the first would be "broken taps." "Other" would be the last grouping for repairs. When collecting data for a Pareto chart, it is useful to have one column labeled "Other." However, if the "Other" column is larger than any of the named categories, you should investigate its content to establish additional groups.

When the data have been collected it is a simple matter to construct the Pareto chart. The causes are listed on the X axis and the

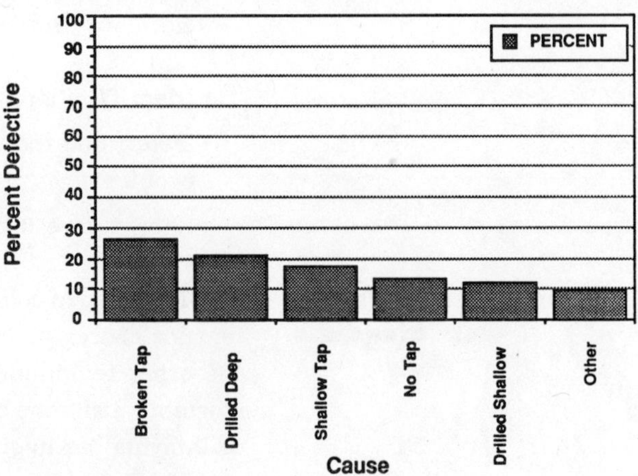

Pareto of Machining Defects (A)

frequency on the Y axis. The categories are then listed in descending order and the bars drawn.

Determining relative seriousness

The Pareto diagram provides a clear picture of how frequently each problem or potential cause of a problem occurs. By reading the height of the bar according to the scale on the left, you can determine how frequently the problem occurs. In our example of all of the repairs made in the department, 26.5 percent are for broken taps. It's also easy to see which problem carries the most weight. This is important from a resourcing point of view. If we are working on solving problems, it's best to work first in areas where the return will be of the greatest benefit.

By adding the percent-of-total line to the Pareto graph, you can quickly see that if we worked on and solved the broken-tap and holes-drilled-deep problems we would eliminate approximately 48 percent of all the machining problems in this department.

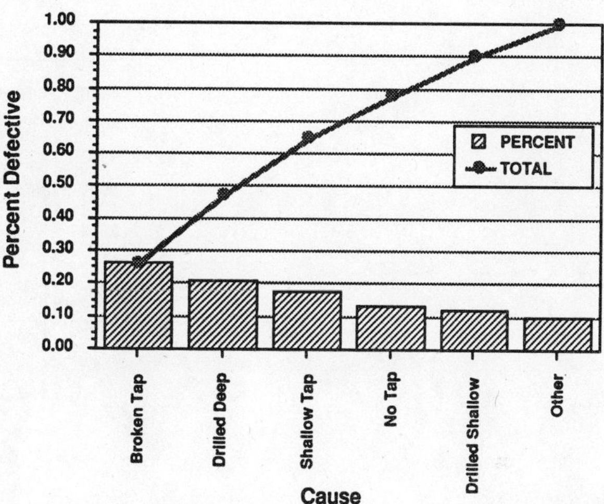

Pareto of Machining Defects (B)

There are times when it is helpful to look at the same information in a different way. This lets us place the resources of the business where they will achieve the greatest return. In our initial data sheet we looked at each repair as a percent of the total repairs. Now we will add the third and fourth dimensions, the cost of making each repair and the total cost of each category. Our new information table now looks like this:

Category	*Frequency*	*Percent of Total*	*Cost of Repair*	*Total Cost*
Other	440	9.7	$2.12	$ 932.80
Broken tap	1200	26.5	1.85	2220.00
No tap	600	13.2	1.02	612.00
Drilled deep	950	21.0	4.35	4132.50
Shallow tap	800	17.6	3.26	2608.00
Drilled shallow	545	12.0	.85	463.25
Totals	4535	100.0		$10,968.55

As a result of looking at the data in a different way we can now see that the real cost to our business is the problem of drilled-deep holes. This can be seen in our next chart.

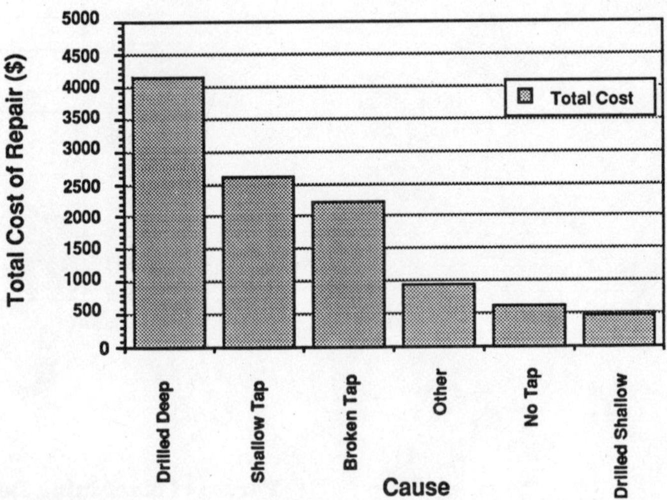

Cost Analysis of Manufacturing Defects

When we compare the two Pareto diagrams we can see that the drilled-deep problem moved from number two to number one when we looked at it from a cost perspective. This tells you that to really reduce your manufacturing costs you should work on and solve the drilled-deep problem first.

Pareto diagrams can also be used to show if improvement has been made. After implementing a corrective action designed to reduce any of the designated problems, you can construct a follow-up diagram to compare the impact of the changes you have made. Note in the Pareto diagram here that holes drilled too deep is no longer listed as a defect.

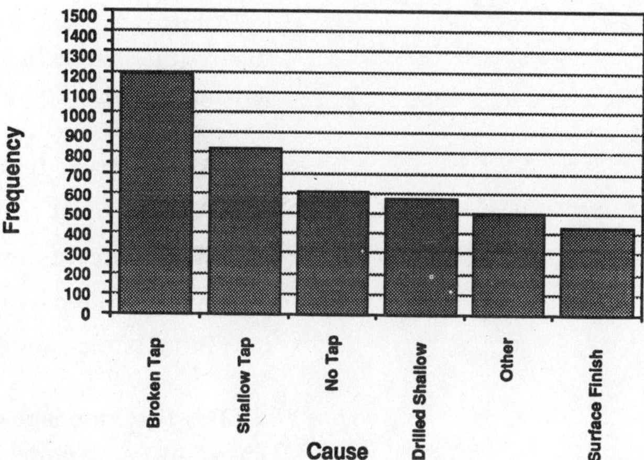

Pareto of Quality Defects, Month 2

A word of caution. What I have found is that for short periods of time we can focus our efforts and contain almost any problem. However, the proof of real resolution is in the monthly Pareto of defects. If the defect fails to resurface, then you can rest assured that you have fixed it.

A Pareto diagram can help you and your team determine the causes or problems that occur most frequently in your area. Reducing the most frequent cause or problem will yield the greatest improvement for your or your team's efforts. I find that determining root cause or solving the biggest problem makes some of the smaller problems disappear as well, because they are usually symptoms of the main problem.

HISTOGRAMS

Histograms, or frequency distributions, are a graphical way of displaying large amounts of data. A histogram normally takes the form of a bar graph when used to display the frequency and range of sample data. Remember, though, a histogram is a view of an operation or process *at one point in time,* and should not be interpreted as the long-term capability of the operation. The bars of the histogram are called "cells." Each cell represents the measurements that fall between the two values. The height of each cell varies according to the number of pieces produced that fell in that value range. By looking at the shape of the cells you can get an idea of what the process is doing at that moment in time.

A histogram is typically used to imply something about the population from which the sample was taken. It will tell you if the sample is normal, bi-modal, skewed, narrow, or spread out. Frequency distributions can give sufficient information about problems to provide the user with the information necessary to start the decision-making process. The end of this section contains graphical examples of the different shapes a histogram can take.

A histogram will also allow you to compare the distribution with the required specifications or standards, and answer some of the following questions:

- Are the parts to print?
- What percent are out of specification?
- What percent are within specification?
- What is the mean of the sample?
- What is the sample's standard distribution?

The first step is to collect and record the data on a data collection sheet—a fancy name for any piece of paper laid out to your specific needs. A general rule of thumb is that you should take a minimum of 30 samples, preferably 50. The actual amount of data collected depends on your particular situation.

Constructing a histogram

All you have to do to construct a histogram is follow these eight steps:

- Step 1. Collect the information to be used (a minimum of 30 samples is suggested, 50 is better).
- Step 2. Locate the minimum and maximum observation, and determine the range.

$$\text{Range} = \text{Maximum} - \text{Minimum}$$

- Step 3. Determine the number of classes by looking in the table. A class is the interval that contains the sample observations. Each observation will be put in one and only one class. The number of classes or cells you should have is somewhat arbitrary. Try to display the data as accurately and as usefully as possible. As a general rule, use the format displayed here.

Histogram
Suggested Class Sizes

Sample Size	Recommended Number of Classes
30 to 45	6 to 8
46 to 90	7 to 9
91 to 180	8 to 10
181 to 375	9 to 11
376 to 750	10 to 12

Class Chart

- Step 4. Obtain the width of the class. This is the numerical distance between boundaries. Class widths should be equal.

Class Width = Range/Number of Classes

The dangers of improperly selected class sizes

The determination of class sizes is the most important single thing you can do when working with histograms. In the next set of examples you will see what happens when you select the class sizes incorrectly. We will use a sample size of 35 (N = 35), and a number set that covers 6.75 to 18.75.

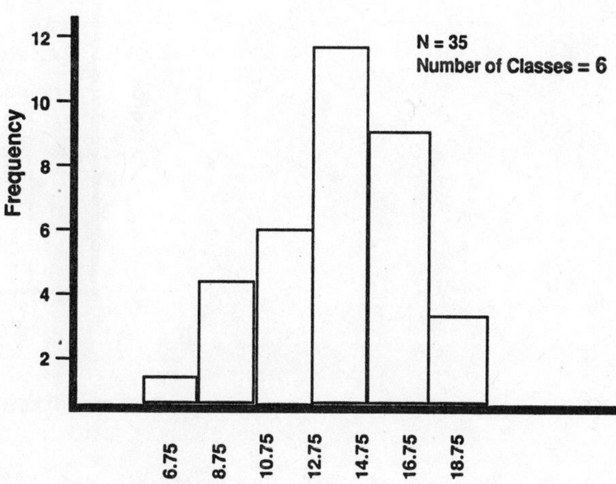

Correct Number of Classes

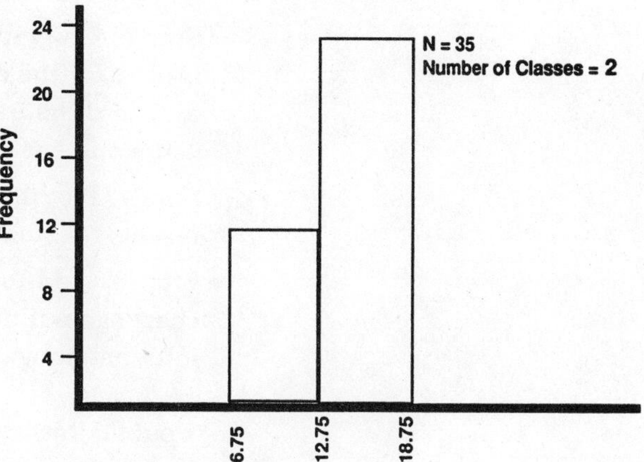

Too Few Class Sizes

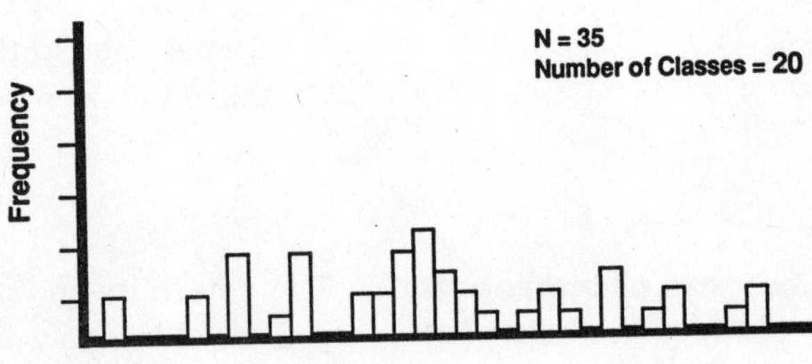

Too Many Classes

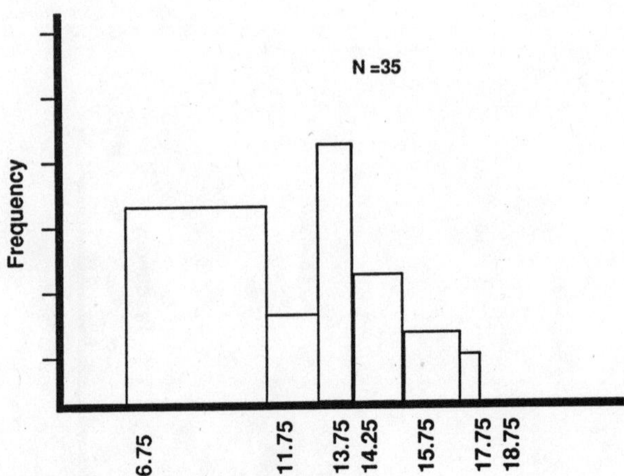

Unequal Class Sizes

- Step 5. Determine the class boundaries and tally the data. Class boundaries are the end points for each class that will classify each observation into exactly one class. The class boundaries of 2.75–3.75 should be used when the data recorded is 2.8, 3.1, 3.3, 2.7. Three is the midpoint of this class.
- Step 6. On graph paper draw a horizontal (or X) axis. This axis is used for the class boundaries. The vertical (or Y) axis is used to record the frequency of occurrence. The frequency of a class is the number of samples that fall within its boundaries.
- Step 7. Plot the data so that the height of each vertical bar represents the number of observations in that class.
- Step 8. Add to the chart the information necessary to do the chart again if necessary. Who, what, when, where, and how the information was collected.

Let's put all this to work. In the example of a flange thickness study shown here we start with 100 samples from a machining operation that milled a block to size.

Date of Study _______

Data										High	Low
3.56	3.46	3.48	3.50	3.42	3.43	3.52	3.49	3.44	3.50	3.56	3.42
3.48	3.56	3.50	3.52	3.47	3.48	3.46	3.50	3.56	3.38	3.56	3.38
3.41	3.37	3.47	3.49	3.45	3.44	3.50	3.49	3.46	3.46	3.50	3.37
3.55	3.52	3.44	3.50	3.45	3.44	3.48	3.46	3.52	3.46	3.55	3.44
3.48	3.48	3.32	3.40	3.52	3.34	3.46	3.43	3.30	3.46	3.52	3.30
3.59	3.63	3.59	3.47	3.38	3.52	3.45	3.48	3.31	3.46	3.63	3.31
3.40	3.54	3.46	3.51	3.48	3.50	3.68	3.60	3.46	3.52	3.68	3.40
3.48	3.50	3.56	3.50	3.52	3.46	3.48	3.46	3.52	3.56	3.56	3.46
3.52	3.48	3.46	3.45	3.46	3.54	3.54	3.48	3.49	3.41	3.54	3.41
3.41	3.45	3.34	3.44	3.47	3.47	3.41	3.48	3.54	3.47	3.54	3.34

all readings in (mm) N =100 High =3.68 Low = 3.30

Collecting the Data

Class No.	Class Boundaries	Mid. Value	Frequency	No.
1	3.276 - 3.325	3.30	xxx	3
2	3.326 - 3.375	3.35	xxx	3
3	3.376 - 3.425	3.40	xxxxx xxxx	9
4	3.426 - 3.475	3.45	xxxxx xxxxx xxxxx xxxxx xxxxx xxxxx xx	32
5	3.476 - 3.525	3.50	xxxxx xxxxx xxxxx xxxxx xxxxx xxxxx xxxxx xx	38
6	3.526 - 3.575	3.55	xxxxx xxxxx	10
7	3.576 - 3.625	3.60	xxx	3
8	3.626 - 3.675	3.65	x	1
9	3.676 - 3.725	3.70	x	1

Generating a Frequency Chart

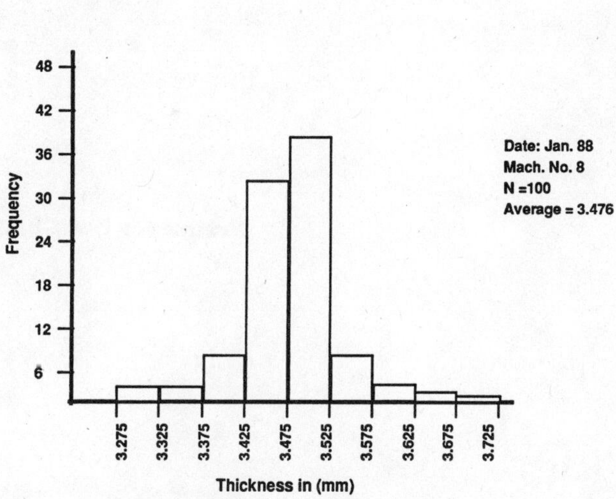

Turning a Frequency Chart into a Histogram

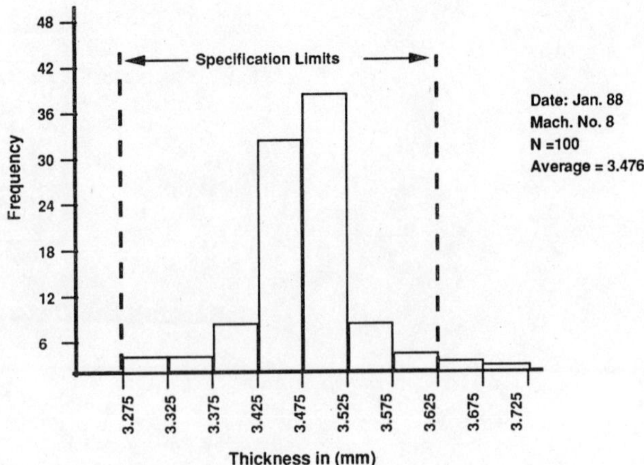

Adding the Specification Limits

Three types of histograms

Histograms come in three basic types: frequency histograms, frequency bar charts, and frequency polygons. These vary only in how they are graphically displayed, as seen here.

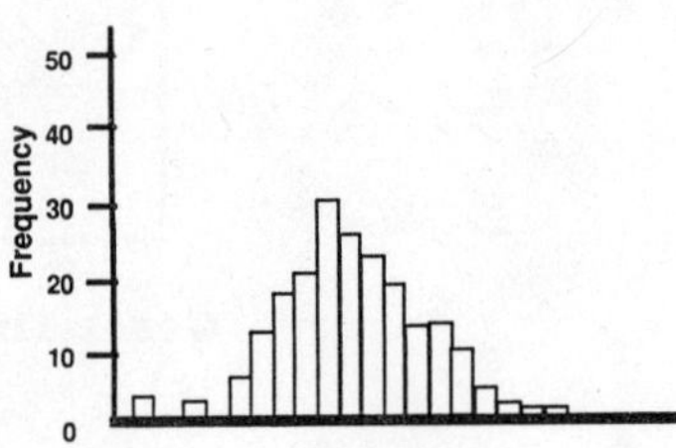

Frequency Histogram

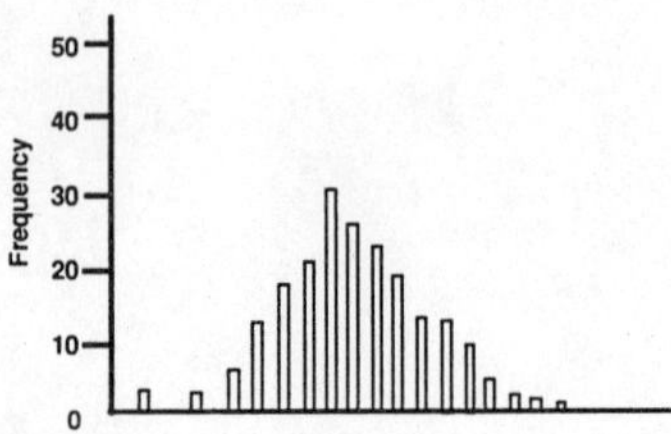

Frequency Bar Chart

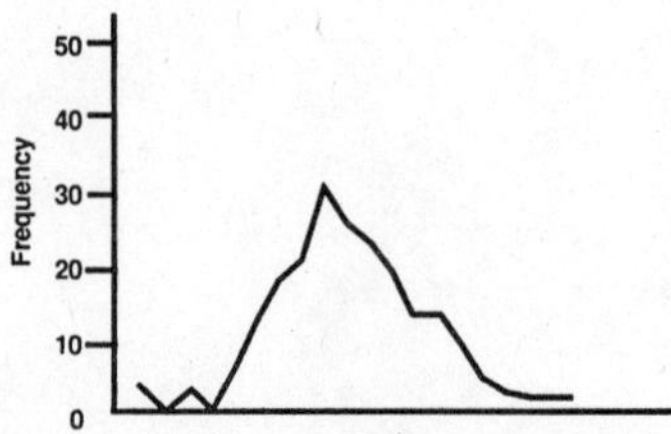

Frequency Polygon

Find the maximum and minimum observation and determine the range.

$$\begin{aligned} \text{Range} &= \text{Maximum} - \text{Minimum} \\ &= 3.68 - 3.30 \\ &= .380 \end{aligned}$$

Find the class size.

$$\begin{aligned} \text{Number of Classes} &= \text{Range}/\#\text{ of classes} \\ &= .380/8 \\ &= .05 \text{ approx.} \end{aligned}$$

Calculate the boundaries.

$$\begin{aligned} \text{Minimum} &= 3.30 \\ \text{Class Size} &= .05 \end{aligned}$$

We will use 3.275 to 3.325 as the first class and continue until we get to 3.725. This can be seen in the histogram below.

Histograms can be misleading

Let's look at the chart below. The upper and lower specification limits of the process are 3 and 12. Looking at this chart, write down what you feel are some of the conclusions you might draw from this data.

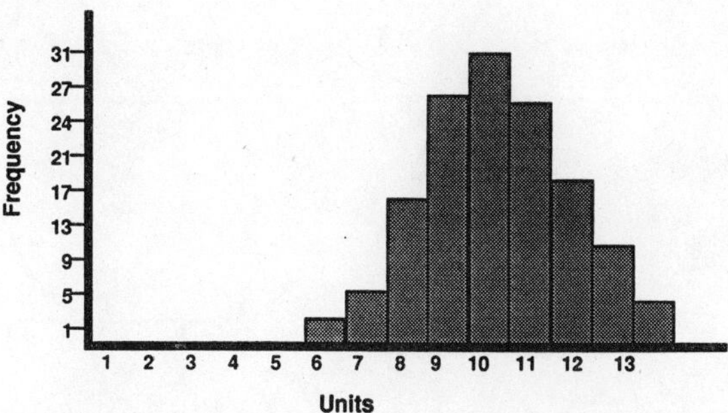

Now let's look at the data that this chart was built off of. What conclusions can you draw from the data, and how does it differ from the chart?

Observation	Sample and Time					
	8:00	9:00	10:00	11:00	1:00	Summary
1	Lower Specification					0
2						0
3	1					0
4	4	1				0
5	1	3				1
6	1	8	2			5
7	1	8	5	2		16
8	3	4	8	6	1	28
9	9	1	6	9	6	32
10	2		3	6	9	27
11	Upper Specification		1	2	7	19
12					2	10
13						2

One of the shortfalls of a histogram is that you cannot see any trends, runs, or cycles. This process is shifting over time, perhaps due to the machine warming up, tool wear, or some other cause. Looking at the histogram would lead you to think that this process is out of control. However, with the addition of a heat exchanger to control the oil temperature, or the initiation of a tool change pro-

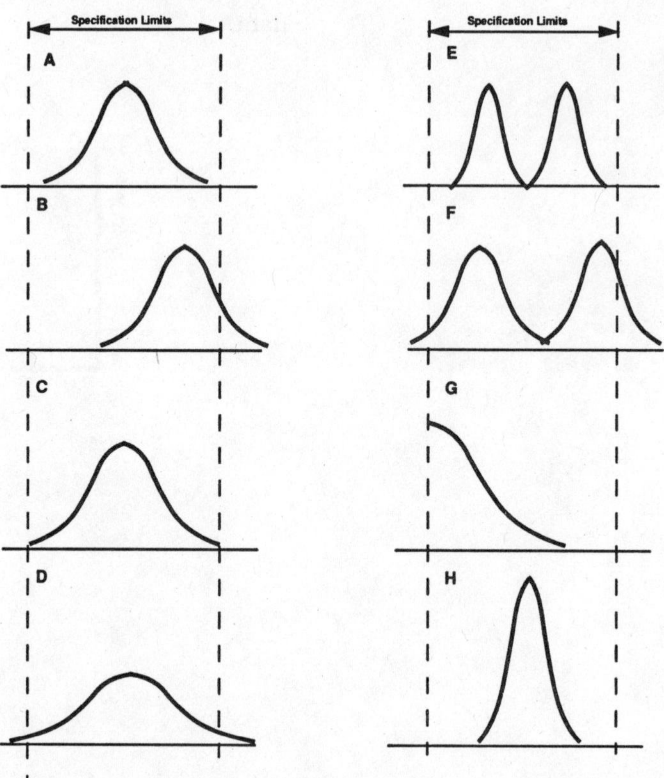

gram, this operation could make all good parts. The lesson to be learned here is that histograms fail to reveal any time-related variability.

Types of process variation a histogram will identify

Each of these shapes tells you something about the data collected. In an attempt to clarify what each shape means, let's define them as they relate to the process or blueprint specification limits:

- *Figure A.* Represents the ideal situation. The range of the distribution is well within the specification limits, and it is centered on the mean.
- *Figure B.* Shows the same distribution, but it has shifted off center enough to be outside the specification limits.
- *Figure C.* In this example the process and specification means are centered. However, the range of the distribution and the specification limits match, a condition that is satisfactory, but it should be watched. Unlike Figure B, it would take only a slight shift in this process to create problems.
- *Figure D.* The range of this distribution is greater than the specification limits.
- *Figure E.* Here we have two separate distributions, both well within the process specification. A situation like this is typical if you have two machines making the same part, or two suppliers.
- *Figure F.* Like Figure E, except that both distributions have a range greater than the specification.
- *Figure G.* A distribution like this is operating outside one of the specification limits. The parts are being inspected 100 percent and those found out of specification are removed from the process.
- *Figure H.* Represents a process that has been problem-solved and some of the variation removed. The range of the distribution has been reduced to the point that, if need be, the process could be safely shifted to accommodate fit and finish requirements.

RUN CHARTS

Run charts will identify:

- Changes in activities.

Run charts will measure:

- Current process performance.
- If an improvement has been made.
- Average process performance.

Run charts are used to visually represent repetitive data. They are used to monitor an operation or system to see whether or not the long-range average is changing.

This makes the run chart a valuable tool in identifying meaningful trends or shifts in the average. When monitoring any system using a run chart, it is expected that you should have an equal number of points above and below the line. This indicates that the system is operating in a steady state. If, however, we have nine consecutive points above or below the current average, you have a "run." This is a statistically unusual event and represents a change in the average.

The danger in using run charts is the tendency to see every variation in data as being important. What we will do now is build a run chart using the daily production reports for one operator. For the employee on operation 10, the production counts for the last 33 days are as follows:

Day	*Production Count*	*Day*	*Production Count*
1	685	18	786
2	728	19	795
3	792	20	804
4	821	21	798
5	785	22	685
6	810	23	745
7	768	24	808
8	545	25	812
9	813	26	819
10	784	27	802
11	775	28	809
12	749	29	798
13	789	30	801
14	796	31	815
15	804	32	809
16	809	33	812
17	798		

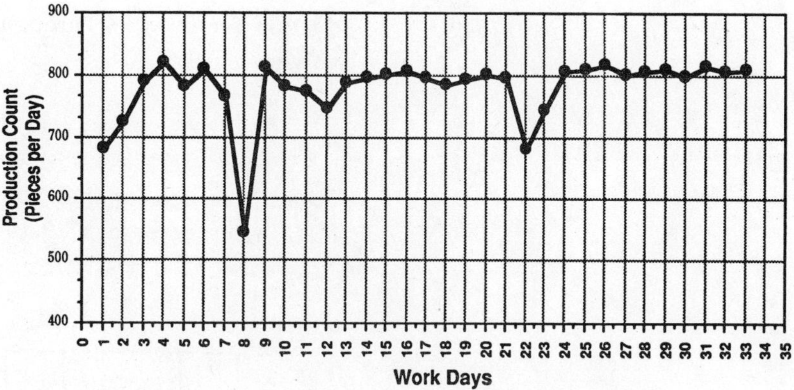

Run Chart of Operator 10's Daily Production Count (A)

Plotting the chart Once you have plotted all of the points on your graph, it is time now to determine the average production for the period in question. This is done by adding up all of the production figures and dividing by the number of days, that is,

$$\text{Total Production/Number of Days} = \text{Average Production}$$
$$25762/33 = 780.66$$

We can now plot the average production on our chart.

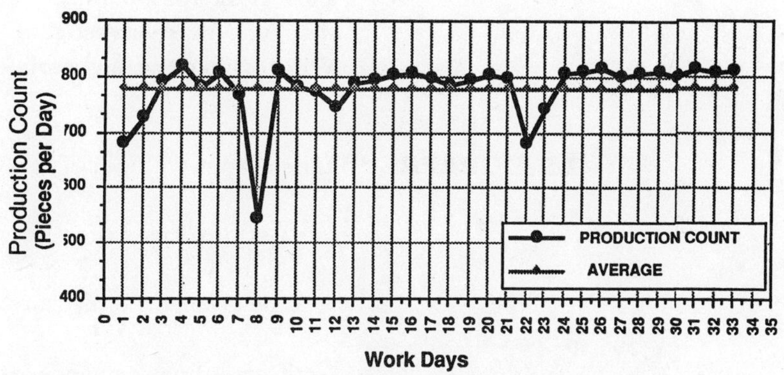

Run Chart of Operator 10's Daily Production Count (B)

If you study the chart, you will see that this chart has the special condition that was pointed out earlier in this section. Note the period starting with day 24; on our data chart we see no production count less than 800. But, visually, it is very apparent that something has happened. All of the points are above the current average.

Using your formula for determining average, find the total production for days 24 through 33, and divide by the total days involved.

$$8098/10 = 809.8$$

So our average for that 10-day period has moved from 780.66 to 809.88, an increase of 29.14 pieces per shift.

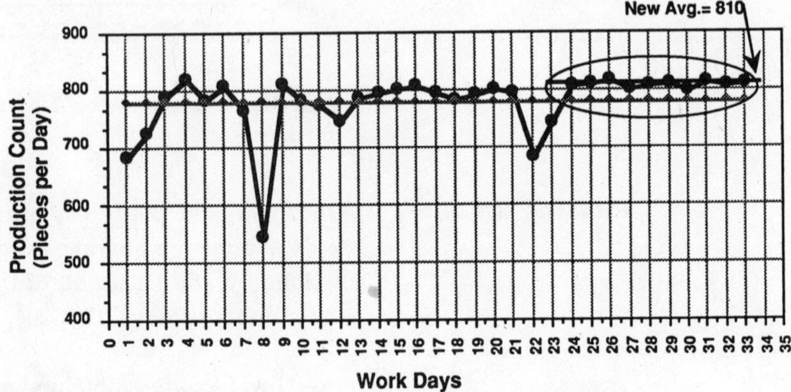

Run Chart of Operator 10's Daily Production Count (C)

The real significance of this move is not the move itself, but *why* the average production count moved from 781 to 810 pieces per shift. If the reason for the shift upward is not immediately apparent, then you must investigate. To determine "Whys," use the "Five Whys" rule described earlier in this chapter.

LINE GRAPHS

Line graphs will identify:

- Performance differences between similar operations.

Line graphs will measure:

- Current performance levels.
- Performance after changes have been made.

Line graphs are helpful when you are tracking similar operations or you are looking for a change in some factor over time, or as a means of comparing the same data from two different sources. If we look at the example here we see that we are comparing the production figures from three identical operations for a period of 20 days. To start, we organize the data in table form much like we have done in many of the other examples.

Day	*Operator 1*	*Operator 2*	*Operator 3*
1	685	798	728
2	728	685	785
3	792	745	745
4	821	808	792
5	785	812	749
6	810	819	775
7	768	802	789
8	545	809	729
9	813	811	685
10	784	801	558
11	775	815	789
12	749	809	788
13	789	812	780
14	796	803	801
15	804	789	800
16	809	798	789
17	798	799	781
18	786	805	800
19	795	806	783
20	804	814	790

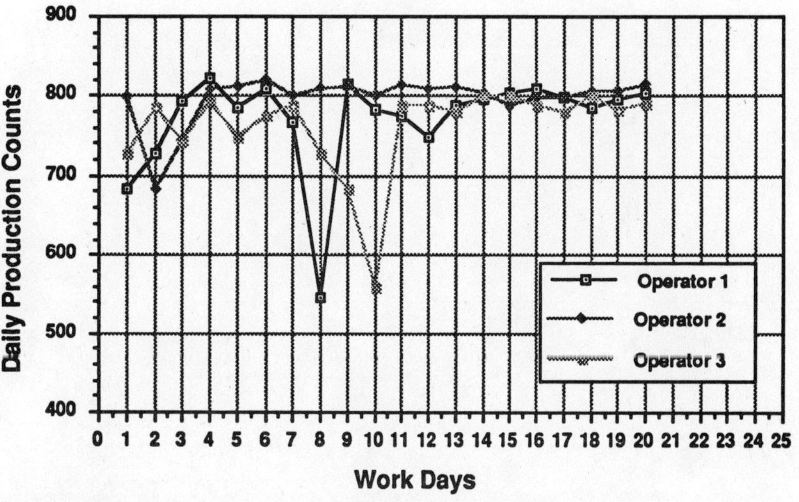

Operator Comparison Chart (Daily Production)

Plotting a line graph

Here we are looking at the variation of production between three operators over a period of 20 days. Some of the things you could do with this chart are:

- Determine the average for the total operation over the 20-day period and plot that line.
- Determine the average for each operator and plot that line.

What you are really looking for by using a chart like this is to reduce the variation between the three operators. By reducing the variation you can help all three shifts work in the same manner, assuring the quality of your products.

SUMMARY

What you have learned in this chapter is how to analyze a problem step by step by first identifying the key ingredients and then systematically finding the root cause. You now recognize that a problem in a manufacturing system is really an out-of-balance condition that exists among those key ingredients—Man, Machine, Method, Material, Measurement, and Environment, all of which, in the right amounts, make for a successful operation.

You understand that the real key to successful problem solving is a plan of how you intend to attack the process to collect the information required. You have learned some simple techniques for discovering which of these may be the one that must be adjusted to regain that important balance. The most important thing to remember is to not become frustrated; you will make mistakes, so learn from them. A good problem solver has the persistence to teach a rock to roll over.

Chapter 5

GENERATE POTENTIAL SOLUTIONS

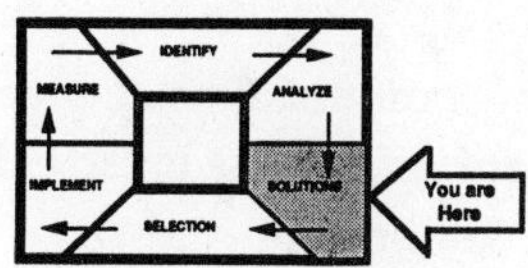

Normally there will be several possible solutions to a problem. The purpose of this step is to assist you in determining the best way to solve the problem you have identified or selected.

Whether you are working alone or in a group, it is important to use all of the creativity you or the group possesses. When working in a group, the same techniques that you used to identify the problem can be used in the generation of its solution. The technique of brainstorming encourages the participants to be creative. The reason for this is that members can build off of each other's ideas. If the rules of brainstorming are followed and the members of the group work together without becoming judgmental, the group will provide an environment for free thinking. The purpose of this chapter is to provide you with the tools necessary to work through the information at hand toward the best solution to the problem.

Let's look at what you have available to assist you in generating potential solutions to your problem. At this point in the process you have:

- A problem statement.
- A goal statement.
- All of the facts you have collected.

The real question is, What do I do with all of this?

ARRIVING AT A SOLUTION

It's at this point in the process that you should stop and review your findings. The best way to begin is to review your original problem statement.

REVIEW THE PROBLEM STATEMENT

You may at this point have enough information about what is happening in the process to confirm your original problem statement, or you may find it necessary to restate the problem. If it is necessary to restate the problem don't feel bad about not having a clear understanding of what was wrong at the outset of the process. Typically, when a thorough investigation is carried out, it may change some or all of the investigator's beliefs about the probable cause of the problem. Don't be afraid to change your statement. During the normal fact-finding process you will have learned more about the problem than you knew at the beginning. This happens all the time. As you gather more information you may find that you did not clearly understand the situation.

The question you must ask at this point is, Does my original problem statement describe the problem as I know it today? This reassessment will help you to clearly understand the situation prior to working out any possible solution.

REVIEW THE GOAL STATEMENT

A thorough knowledge of the problem has the same impact on the goal statement as it does on the problem statement. When originally written, the goal may have been clear. However, as investigation of a problem brings about a clearer understanding, that gained knowledge may change the direction you must go to resolve the problem.

In other words, after a thorough investigation, you may determine that your original goal was understated, or overly aggressive. The real challenge that faces some people at this point is the admission that they may have made a mistake.

It is helpful at this point to remember that, properly used, this problem-solving process is a learning experience, and as such it is O.K. to make a mistake. Also, recognizing that in some organizations mistakes are not tolerated, we know that it is in these organizations that problems are swept under the carpet. It is also characteristic in these organizations that costs are normally out of control. People fail to contribute, and nothing ever seems to get done.

Changing direction may look something like this: Let's say that in your original statement your goal had been to reduce the number of undrilled holes due to broken tooling by 30 percent. But with a better understanding of the problem and the potential causes of broken tooling, you now feel it is possible to reduce the number of holes not drilled due to broken tooling by 50 percent. To do this you must have a clear understanding of the potential causes of the problem. Remember, in a manufacturing operation, the solving of problems relates directly to dollars saved. It is better to have a goal that is attainable. Unattainable goals only lead to personal and organizational frustration.

WORKING OUT SOLUTIONS

We must understand that most problems have more than one solution and most solutions require several incremental steps to put them in place. I will break the generating of possible solutions into two fields. First we will address the solution as a whole. Then we will look at the incremental steps that make up that solution. What we will do is attempt to demonstrate a method of proof testing both prior to the implementation.

ANALYZING DATA

When you have collected your raw data, you should display and analyze it. Again, there are many techniques. In this chapter are some of the methods of analyzing and displaying quantitative data.

TYPES OF SOLUTIONS

When we look at what it will take to solve the kinds of problems normally found in the manufacturing situation, we can divide the solutions into two types, operation-specific and multi-operation.

Please do not get the selection and the implementation processes confused. When I talk about selecting the best solution it does not mean that there is only one way to implement it. Whether the problem is focused or requires action from more than one area of the business to solve it, there is normally more than one way to implement the final fix.

Machine, or operation-specific solutions

These are solutions that will be focused on one specific machine or operation in your manufacturing system. Solving this type of problem will force you to focus all of your efforts on one specific area of your operation. You will focus on a specific machine or assembly method to improve its performance. In any case, your efforts will be concentrated in a very small area of the total operation.

Multi-operation solutions

These kinds of problems will require action to be taken in more than one area of the manufacturing system. Here we are looking at solutions that will require the coordinated effort of several areas in order to bring about a solution. Solutions of this type typically involve engineering changes, material changes, or product design changes in order to resolve them.

LISTING ALL POSSIBLE SOLUTIONS

There will more than likely be more than one solution to your problem. The old quote, "There's more than one way to skin a cat," was spoken by an enlightened problem solver. The real challenge is to find the "best" solution, which is always the simplest one: simple to understand, simple to implement, and worked on by all of the concerned parties. This is the solution that will work.

TESTING YOUR SOLUTIONS

This is the point in the process where you will begin to ask yourself the "What if" questions. To assist you in developing answers to these questions, I have included in this chapter some helpful tools. They are simple things that you can do and use: the truth matrix, median scatter plots, multi-vari diagrams, scale drawings, and location plots.

Remember, the solution should be as simple as possible.

TESTING YOUR IDEAS ON PAPER

Prior to moving into the selection process, first test your top three or four ideas on paper. The ideas presented here in some cases can be used both to analyze the problem and to test the proposed ideas for solution. The idea here is to narrow down the selection process to two or three possible solutions.

TOOLS TO HELP YOU ANALYZE

- The truth matrix will identify any problems in the solution.
- The truth matrix will measure your potential for success.

THE TRUTH MATRIX

The truth matrix is simply a test circuit for your proposed method of solving the problem. It involves breaking down the proposed solution into the incremental steps that would be required to implement the idea and then determining whether, if that step were to be carried out, it really would contribute to the solution of the problem. As you can see in the example, the first thing to do is to write down the proposed first step in the solution of the problem.

Solution Statement	Anticipated Results	Truth
		Yes - No
		Yes - No

Truth Matrix (A)

Next, write down the anticipated results if that statement is followed through to completion. Finally, the tough part, honestly evaluate the results.

Solution Statement	Anticipated Results	Truth
Redesign the holding fixture on station 3a of the rough drilling machine	This will provide the additional support required to achieve the support required to drill the hole in the proper position	(Yes) - No
Provide the operator with additional training	This will assist the operator in making sure the job is done correctly each time	Yes - (No)

Truth Matrix (B)

As you work through the various steps required to bring the problem to solution, you may find that you are getting more "no" answers than "yes" answers. If so, you can more than likely set the suggested solution aside.

MULTI-VARI DIAGRAMS

Multi-vari diagrams will identify:

- Piece-to-piece variation.
- Variation over time.
- Variation within the piece.
- Variation from different process streams.

Multi-vari diagrams will measure:

- Improvements made to the process.

Multi-vari diagrams may not reveal the cause of your problem, but they will tell you where the problem is, and if you are on the right track toward correcting it. The multi-vari chart is a tool to be used both to determine the problem and to generate and test possible solutions. The multi-vari chart was developed to deal with problems that are multi-dimensional.

As in nature, it is a fact in any manufacturing process that no two pieces are made exactly alike. No two natural things or creatures of the same category are the same. The variation may be so small that it is not noticeable to the eye, or it may be so large that it is easily identifiable. For example, how many people in your family are exactly the same height? The same holds true for a manufacturing process. Even though they are produced on the same machines, parts will vary. The variation may be very small, or the parts may appear to be identical; in these cases better or more-accurate measuring equipment will identify the differences. You must be able to measure accurately before the process can be corrected or controlled.

Four types of variation

- *Variation within the piece.* This type of variation can be found when you look at the taper in the diameter of a ground shaft, or the width of a milled slot, or the surface finish of a ground surface.
- *Variation from piece to piece.* Variation of this type can be seen when you measure parts that have been made one after the other; for example, measuring a specific dimension on five consecutive parts made on any production line.
- *Variation from time to time.* Variation of this type can be observed by looking at parts produced at different times of the day, week, month, or year. Parts made in the morning may be differ-

ent from those made in the afternoon due to the machine warming up, tools wearing, or in the case of exhaustive manual labor, operator fatigue. Batch runs made at different times fall into this category. Big swings in temperature from summer to winter can also cause problems.

- *Variation from process stream to process stream.* This type of variation is typical where you have two or more processes producing the same part or product. Statistically, this would be the same as a bimodal distribution.

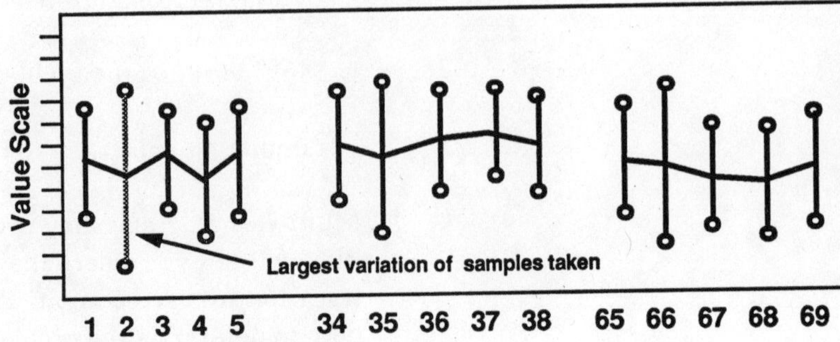

Variation Within the Piece

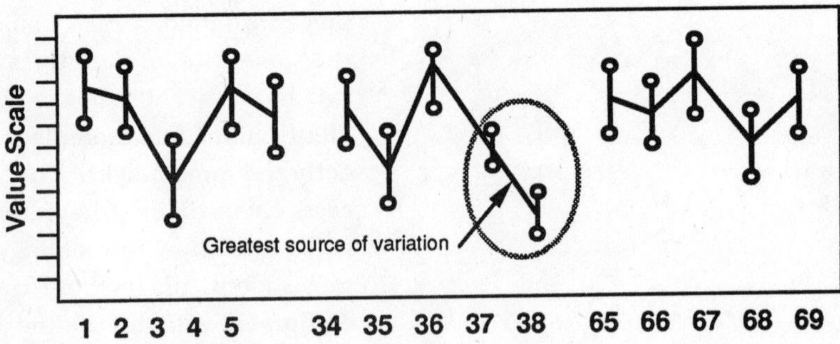

Piece-to-Piece Variation

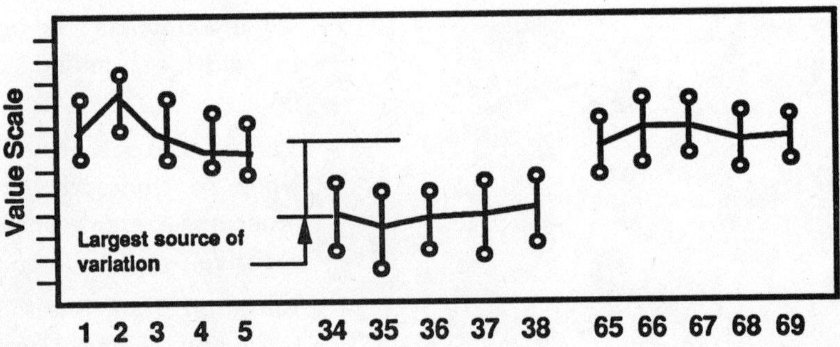

Time-to-Time Variation

The multi-vari diagram will tell you the type of variation that is contributing to your problem. It allows you to see if progress is being made when ideas are put into place.

Developing a multi-vari diagram

For our example, we will use a piston used in a pump assembly. As you can see from the illustration, the tolerances are extremely close. What we are looking for are any conditions that would not allow us to manufacture the part to its specified dimensions.

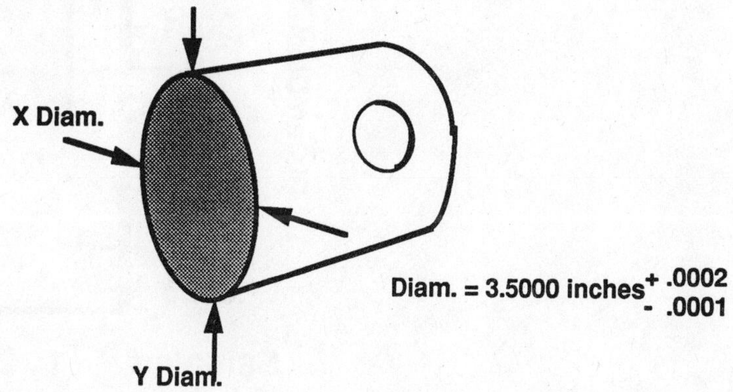

The first step is to collect five consecutive samples and measure them in both directions (X and Y axes). It is helpful to chart the information prior to plotting it on the multi-vari diagram. The reading we are showing here is the amount plus or minus from nominal that the part reads on our gage.

The next step is to begin plotting your finding on the diagram. First, plot the reading for the X axis. In our example, this is −.0001.

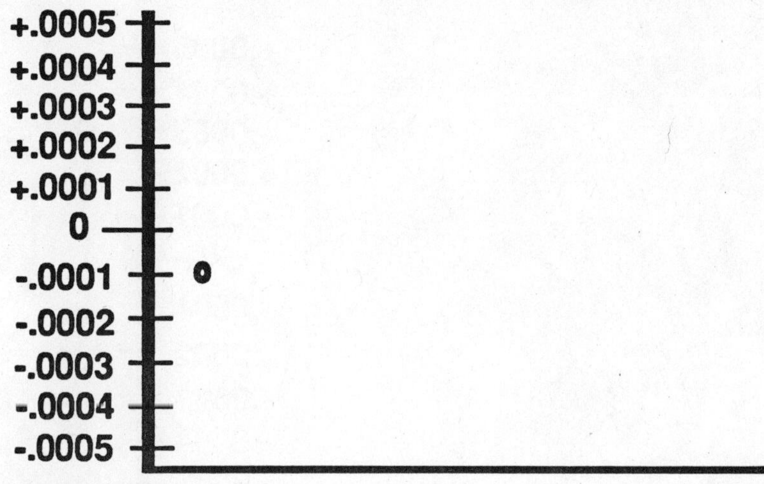

Multi-Vari Diagram (A)

Next, plot the Y axis reading directly above or below the X axis reading, then connect the points with a straight line. The length of the line is the amount of the out-of-round condition existing in this part.

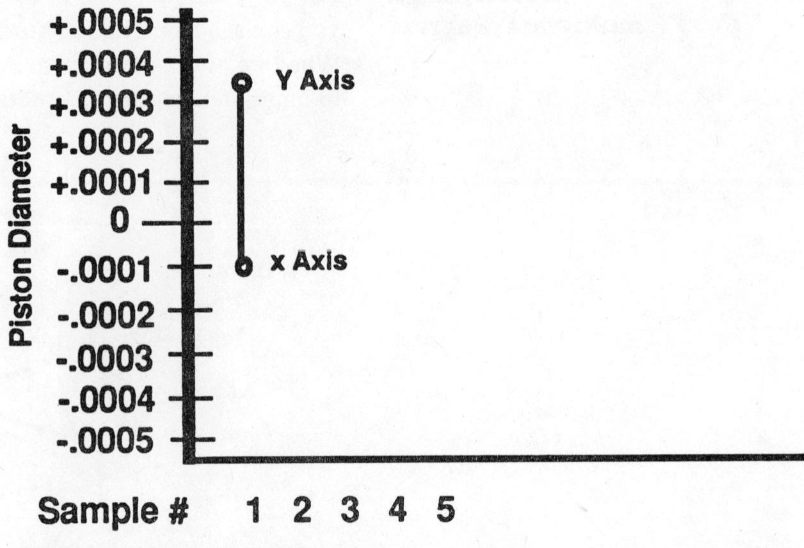

Multi-Vari Diagram (B)

Follow the same procedure for all of the samples taken. Looking at our diagram you can see that our first sample piece is more out-of-round than any of the other samples. This plot gives us an idea of the variation that takes place within the piece. Our diagram shows us that pieces 1, 4, and 5 are outside of our specifications, and that part #2 is marginally acceptable. The only good part in our first sample is part #3.

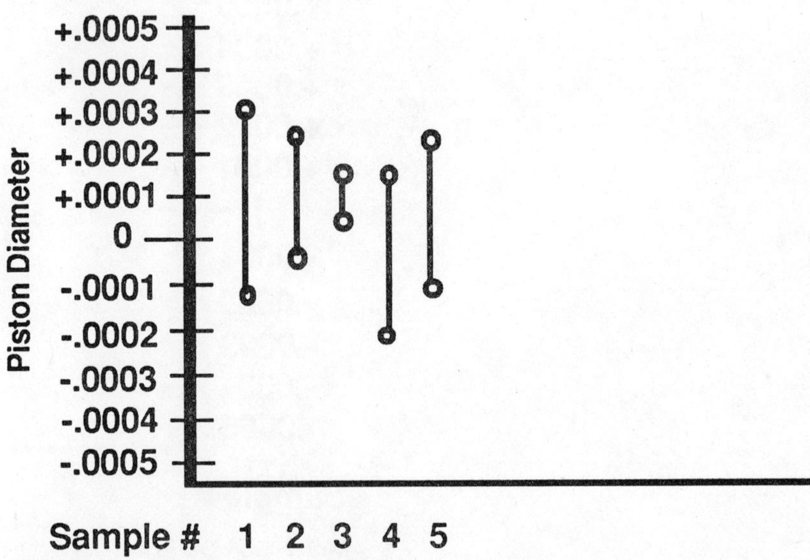

Multi-Vari Diagram (C)

The next step is to connect the mid-point of each piece. This is an indicator of piece-to-piece variation.

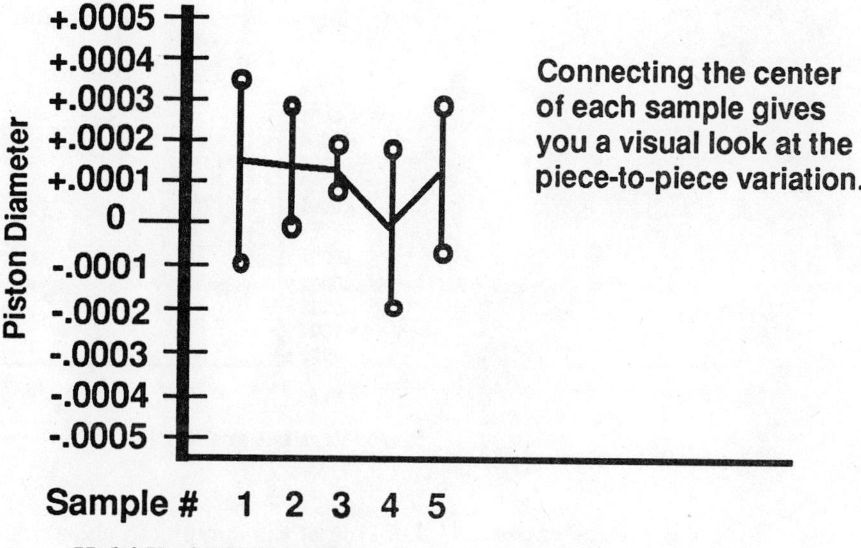

Multi-Vari Diagram (D)

Collect and plot additional samples in the same manner as you did with the first.

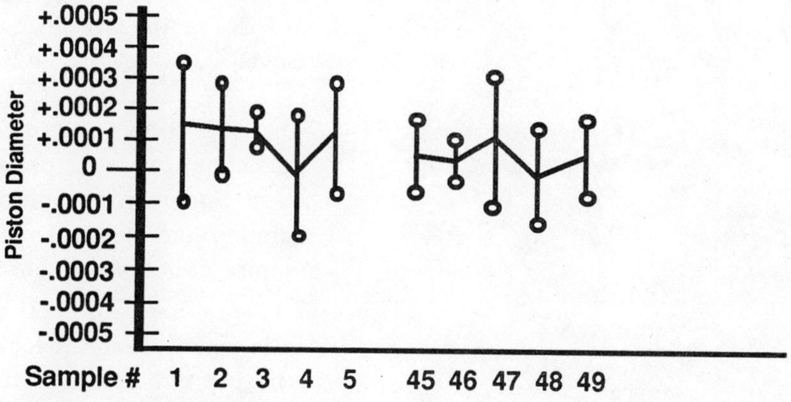

Multi-Vari Diagram (E)

Collect and plot as many additional samples as you feel are necessary to give you what is felt to be a representative sample of the operation. When the samples have been collected and plotted on your diagram, you can then begin the interpretation process.

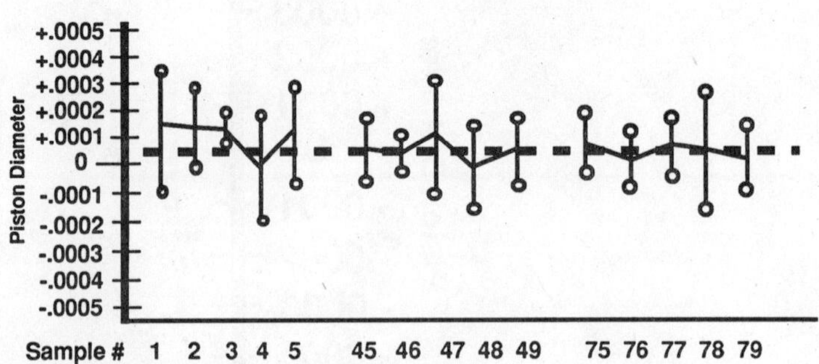

Multi-Vari Diagram (F)

Analyzing a multi-vari diagram

Looking at the completed chart you will see that time-to-time variation is present. The out-of-round condition is not constant over time. The later samples show a reduction in the average out-of-round condition. The average of the samples has also dropped from sample to sample. Some of the probable causes of this condition might be inconsistent clamping pressure, material changes, or inconsistent RPM on the spindle, or the oil temperature may affect all of the above.

Questions about multi-vari diagrams

- What size sample should be taken?

  Minimum number of samples is three, with a maximum of seven. Under normal operation, five samples are preferable. Remember, like statistics, an odd number is better than an even number. It is easier to get a median using an odd number.

- Do I take the samples at the same time every day?

  No, in an attempt to look at the time-to-time variation as well as the piece-to-piece variation, it is essential to plan when to take your samples. If you plan to sample for a period of two days, take samples at different times on each of the days. The time selected should allow you to gain a complete picture of the process over time.

- How frequently do I sample?

  Under normal conditions three times per shift is sufficient. If it is a high-output operation, or has frequent tool changes, then more samples should be taken.

- How many days do I take samples?

  Under normal conditions two days is plenty. If for some reason you have unscheduled work stoppages during that period, then simply extend your sampling into the third day.

Remember, by measuring different points on the piece, and measuring consecutive pieces at various times, you can learn a lot about your process. The following chart shows the different types of variation that can be found in the samples that you will take. Within the piece you may see up to four different types of variation, and then there is piece-to-piece and time-to-time variation as well to consider.

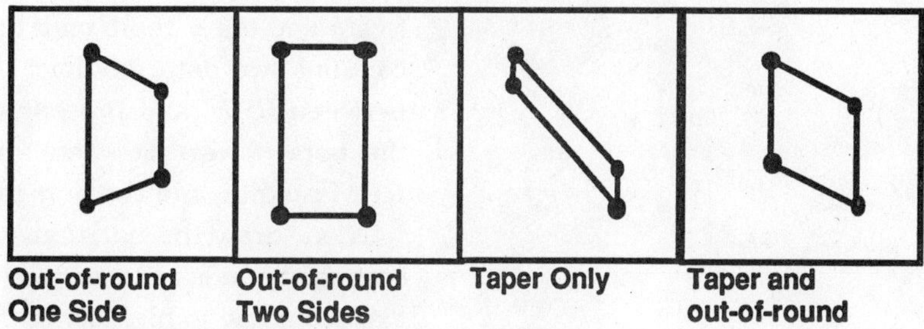

Types of Variation Found Within a Piece

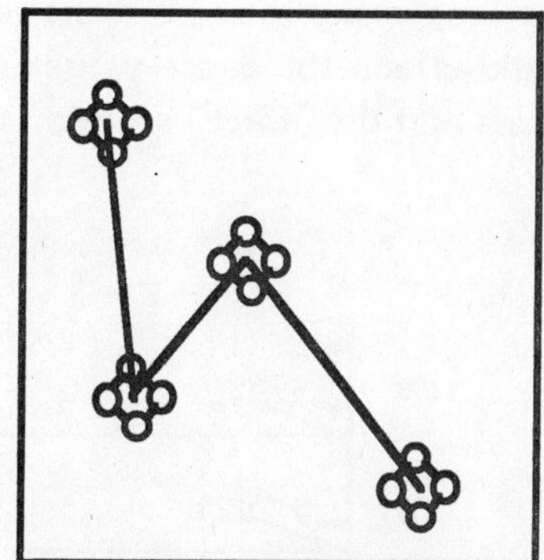

Piece-to-Piece Variation

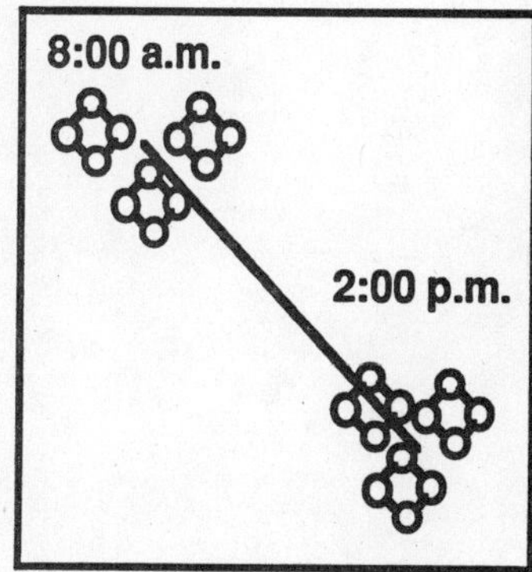

Time-to-Time Variation

For additional information on multi-vari diagrams, see the reference book *Quality Planning and Analysis* by Juran and Gryna.

MEDIAN SCATTER DIAGRAMS

Scatter diagrams will identify:

- The effect one variable has on another.

Scatter diagrams will measure:

- The relationship one variable has on another.
- The numerical effect of change.

Scatter diagrams are used to study the relationship between one variable and another. They are used to test for possible cause-and-effect relationships. A scatter diagram cannot prove that one variable "causes" the other, but it can make it clear that a relationship does exist.

A scatter diagram is set up so that the horizontal axis represents a value for one of the variables, and the vertical axis represents the other variable. A typical scatter diagram is shown below.

The first step in developing a scatter diagram is to collect between 60 and 100 paired data sets whose relationships you wish to investigate and enter them on a data sheet. A paired data set is one that contains two data readings. An example would be the relationship between RPM and horsepower. The higher the RPM, the greater the horsepower. To correlate this data you would need both the RPM reading and the horsepower.

Next, draw the horizontal and vertical axes of the graph. When scaling the axes, the standard practice is to scale the vertical or Y axis from low to high using the point of intersection with the X axis as the start point. The horizontal axis is normally scaled from low to high using the same point of intersection as the start point. When possible, make the length of both axes the same so that the diagram will be easier to read. If the relationship of the data is that of cause-and-effect, the cause values are normally placed on the horizontal axis and the effect values on the vertical axis.

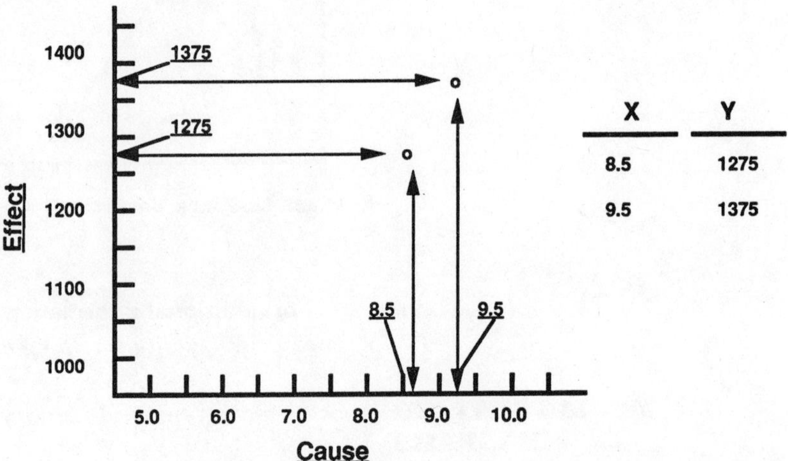

Notice how the plotted points form a pattern. The direction and tightness of this pattern gives you a clue to the strength of the relationship between the two variables. The more the cluster resembles a straight line the stronger the relationship or correlation the two variables have. This means that every time one of the variables changes, the other would change by the same amount.

Measuring relationship

How do we measure the relationship of the two independent incidents? We do so by reading the scatter diagram looking for signs of correlation. Below are some of the various patterns and meanings that a scatter diagram can have.

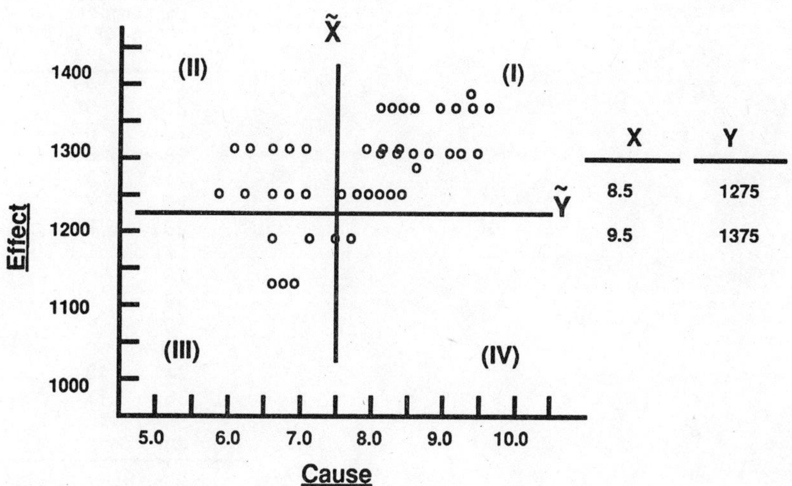

Mark the four areas created when we placed the median lines on the chart I, II, III, and IV, starting in the upper right-hand corner and moving counterclockwise. When this is completed, count the number of points in each area and the points on the line and list them on a summary chart.

Summary Chart

Area	Points
(I)	
(II)	
(III)	
(IV)	
On the Line	
Total	

Summary Chart

Now, to determine the number of points in areas II and IV ("N"), take the total number of points and subtract the number of points on the line.

Compare the total number of points in areas II and IV with the "limit of number of points" column indicated in the Sign Test Table. If the number of points of the two areas is less than the limited numbers, a correlation exists.

N	LIMIT OF NUMBER OF POINTS FOR I+III, II=IV	N	LIMIT OF NUMBER OF POINTS FOR I+III, II=IV
20	5	42	14
21	5	44	15
22	5	46	15
23	6	48	16
24	6	50	17
25	7	52	18
26	7	54	19
27	7	56	20
28	8	58	21
29	8	60	21
30	9	62	22
32	9	64	23
34	10	66	24
36	11	68	25
38	12	70	26
40	13		

Note: This table is limited to N = 20 - 70 at a 5% level of significance

Sign Test Table

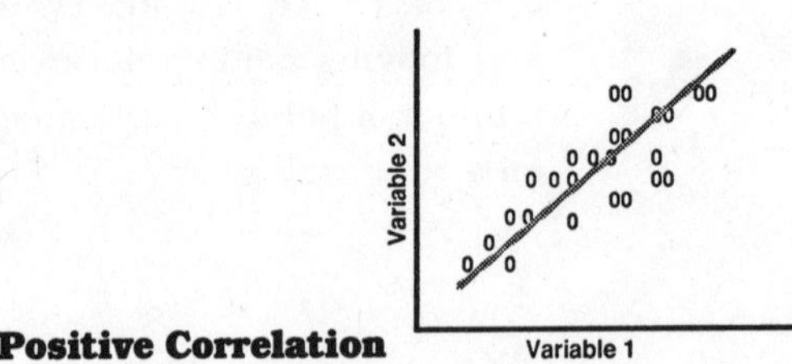

Positive Correlation

A *positive correlation* means that an increase in the value of X results in an increase in the value of Y. It also means that if you control the value of X, you can control the value of Y.

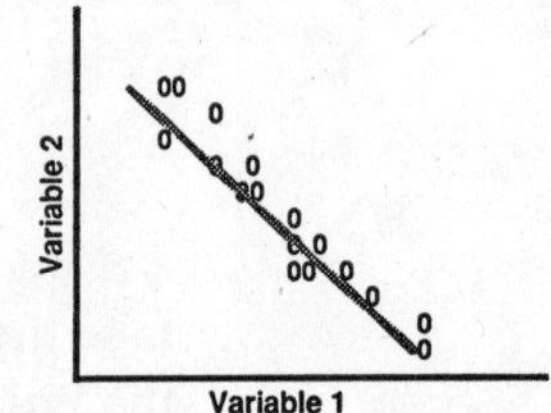

Negative Correlation

A *negative correlation* means that an increase in X will cause a decrease in Y. Therefore, as in the preceding example, if we control X, Y will be controlled naturally.

No Correlation

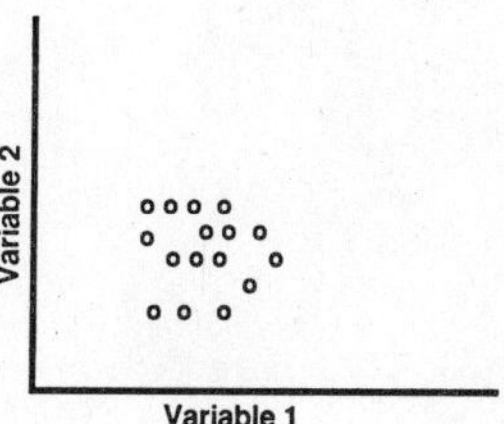

No correlation means just what it says. The values of X and Y mean nothing to each other.

The construction of a scatter diagram is simple:

- Collect the data.
- Draw and label the axes.
- Plot the data.
- Test for correlation.

Testing for correlation

The method described, the so-called median method for analyzing correlations, is the most practical one for our application. The first step is to find the median of the X and Y axes by placing the data in rank order. The next step is to count down from the top to find the middle data set. In our case the median is 7.5 and 1037 respectively.

	X	*Y*
	6.0	1020
	6.5	1021
	7.0	1032
	7.5	1037
	8.0	1040
	8.5	1041
	8.1	1045
Median	7.50	1037

Remember, the scatter diagram is best used when you need to display the relationship of variables or the control one variable might have over another. This can be demonstrated by measuring the change or influence the variables have on each other. If one of them changes, what happens to the other? It will prove or disprove their relationship to each other.

EXERCISE

The problem you are faced with is to show your son or daughter that the time spent studying really does improve their grade point average. To accomplish this task you went to the local school and collected the following data. The two things you looked at were the percent correct on the tests versus the time spent studying for the test. The data is as follows:

Sample #	*Percent Correct*	*Study Time (hrs.)*
1	7	.5
2	62	2.5
3	35	2.5
4	80	6.0
5	92	6.0
6	80	3.5
7	32	3.0
8	82	3.0
9	50	1.0
10	25	1.0
11	60	2.0
12	35	2.0
13	50	2.5
14	70	2.0
15	45	4.0
16	90	4.0
17	91	3.5
18	72	3.5
19	74	4.5
20	86	4.5
21	97	4.5
22	30	.5
23	25	0.0
24	42	1.0
25	75	5.0
26	93	5.0
27	90	4.0
28	60	3.5
29	82	5.5
30	90	5.5
31	74	4.5

Using the example problem, determine if there is any correlation between study time and test scores.

SCALE DRAWINGS

Scale drawings will identify:

- The relationship of one thing to another.

Scale drawings will measure:

- The size relationship of things.
- Clearances or interferences.
- Relative size of objects to each other.

Scale drawings are an essential tool in looking for a possible solution to your problem, as we were able to see in the workstation design layout of the work area. Scale drawings also help in other areas, such as tool layouts and floor plans. These are helpful in visualizing what would really happen if we put our solution in place. There is a saying, "It is cheaper to do it on paper." To prove this I will use one of my favorite examples, which I call a location plot.

LOCATION PLOTS

Location plots will identify:

- Current location of objects.
- Current surface profile.
- Location of mating holes.

Location plots measure

- Exact location of objects.
- Exact profile of surfaces.
- Any changes made.

What we are attempting to do with the location plot is to determine where an existing hole or surface is. To accomplish this, simply draw a plot diagram that resembles a target. The center of the target represents the nominal location, or the zero set for the hole or surface being charted. The scale used on the X and Y axes should relate to the gages you are using to measure the parts. In other words, don't scale the diagram in ten-thousandths increments when the gage reads out only in thousands. As you can see in Location Plot (A), we have scaled the diagram in .001 increments.

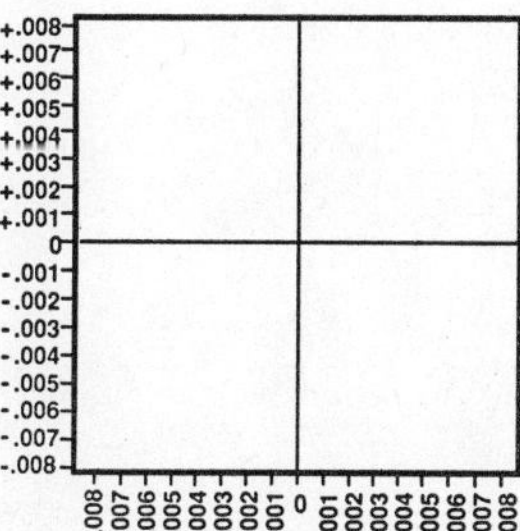

Location Plot (A)

The next step in the development of your location plot is to take five consecutive readings to determine the current location of the hole or plane you are working on.

X	*Y*
−.006	−.004
−.006	−.0045
−.005	−.005
−.004	−.004
−.0045	−.005

Now plot the five points on the location plot diagram. The results should look like Location Plot (B).

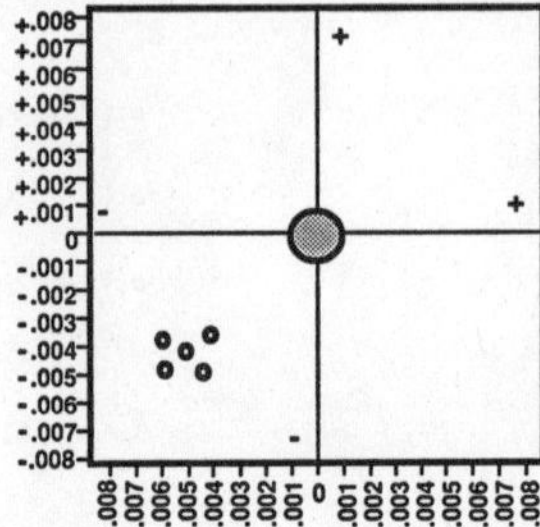

Location Plot (B)

The next step is to determine the average for both the X and Y axes and to plot that point on the chart. The average is determined by adding up the values of X and Y and dividing by the total number of readings for each. In our example that would be five.

	X	*Y*
	−.006	−.004
	−.006	−.0045
	−.005	−.005
	−.004	−.004
	−.0045	−.005
Total =	−.0255	−.0225
Avg. =	−.0051	−.0045

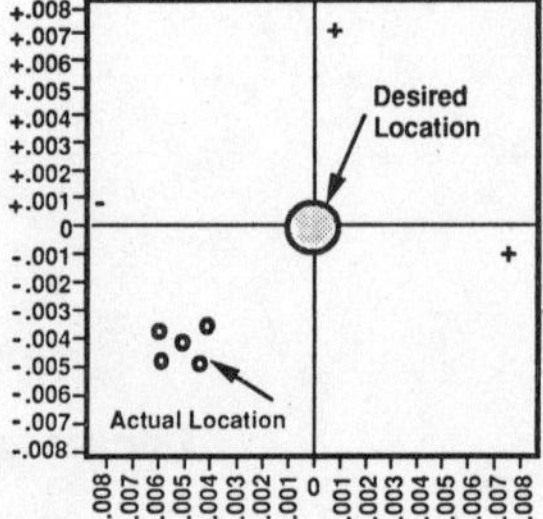

Location Plot (C)

So, for our example, the X plot will be −.0051, and the Y plot will be a −.0045. This represents the distance from the nominal location where the operation is currently positioning the holes.

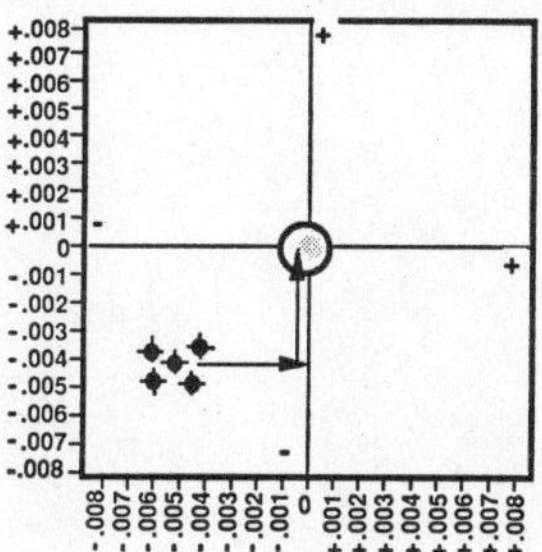

Location Plot (D)

Location Plot (E) represents an operation that is in serious trouble. If during your data gathering you see data that looks like this after it is plotted, you can be sure that the problem does not lie in the operation you are dealing with—unless that operation is that you are attempting to do precision work with a hand drill.

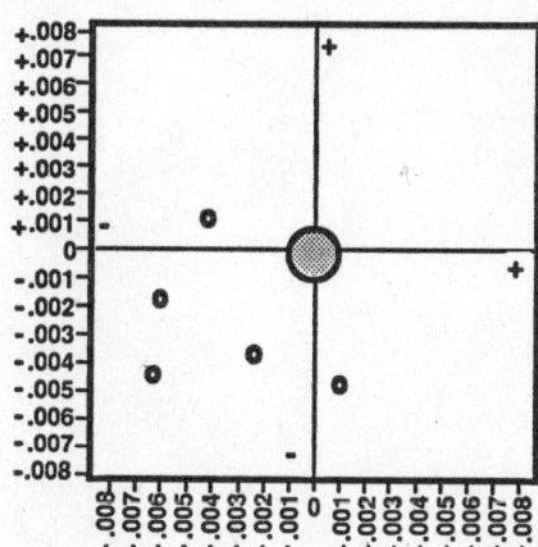

Location Plot (E)

There are other uses for the location plot. One is when you are attempting to align mating holes in component parts. The example shown here demonstrates how this would be used. As you can see,

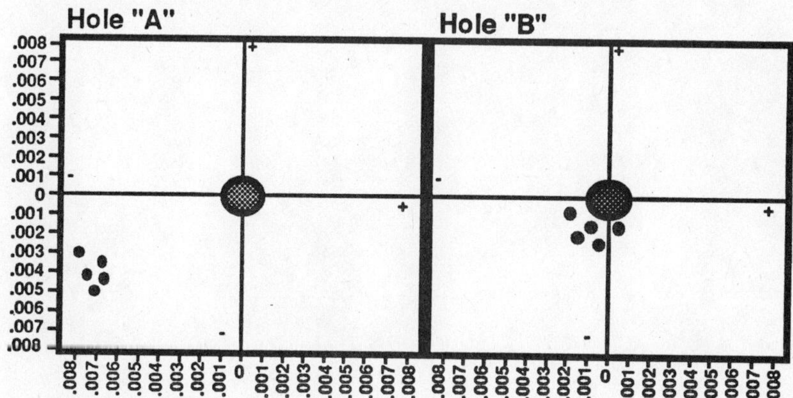

Location Plot for Alignment

there is a location problem between holes "A" and "B." By using the techniques explained above, the two holes can be repositioned so that the assembly operation can take place.

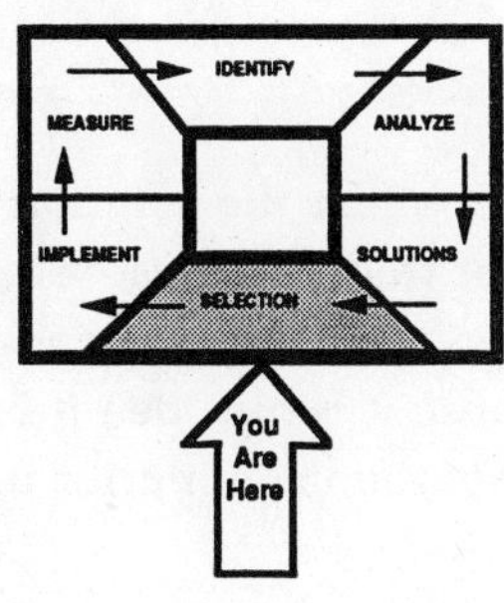

Chapter 6

THE SELECTION PROCESS

In the previous step you generated some possible solutions to the problem. Now you must select which one(s) you think will best solve it.

If you are working individually you should consult with a friend, or better yet someone who will understand what you are trying to accomplish, prior to making your choice. If you are working in a group, discuss all of the potential solutions and reach a consensus about the one(s) you will choose. You will also want to involve any other individuals who might have a stake in the possible solutions, for example, managers and operators, at this stage in the process. The reason for this is simple: they are the groups who will ultimately agree to provide the necessary resources.

In either situation it is important to be clear about the criteria that will determine your final choice of solution(s).

SUGGESTED CRITERIA

CONTROL

The first criterion is the extent to which you control the solution to the problem and the events required to bring about the solution. This was explained in Chapter 2 where types of problems you would be faced with were defined. The same definitions apply here.

- A Type I problem is one over which you have very little or no control or ability to influence any part of it. This makes implementing a solution extremely difficult.
- A Type II problem is one over which the people involved in the solution have the ability and authority and skills to implement the solution.
- A Type III problem is one that requires that the individual or group go outside their immediate work group to seek help. They may lack one of the key ingredients necessary in solving a Type II problem ability, authority, or skill. This forces them to look outside.
- A Type IV problem is one for which you can only report on possible solutions. You must rely entirely on others to implement the solution you select. Typically, this is the most frustrating of all the types.

RELEVANCE

Relevance refers to the degree to which the solution will actually solve the problem. It's at this point that you must refer back to the truth matrix in Chapter 5. Were you completely honest? There are times when we feel that just because it is our idea it is the only solution to the problem. Study the solution again prior to committing.

SERIOUSNESS

How serious is the problem? If it does not get fixed, what will the impact be? If it is a safety- or quality-related issue, the need to fix the problem is great. On the other hand, if it is a cost-related issue the sense of urgency to fix the situation may not carry the same priority. Yes, there *are* times when businesses are not in a position to spend money to make money, primarily because they don't have the money to spend. So, please be sensitive to that condition, but don't get discouraged. Suggest that the idea be put in the "things-to-do" file.

TIME TO SOLVE

How much of your time or the time of others will be required to develop a successful solution to this problem? Time is one of the more costly and valuable resources of a business, and it relates to the degree of difficulty required to implement a solution. In this area, it may be more effective to take small incremental steps than to plunge headlong into something that could potentially have a negative outcome.

RETURN ON INVESTMENT

What is the expected payback if the problem is solved? The payback of safety-related issues cannot be measured in dollars, so in cases of safety this criterion does not apply. But in cases of quality and cost projects, ROI plays an important part. The proper way to present this is in terms of "what the savings are" and not in the negative sense of "what it will cost."

The return can be measured in both dollars and customer satisfaction. Solutions addressing customer satisfaction can be viewed as subjective and so must have strong support data, that is, warranty claims, customer surveys, product returns for specific reasons, and so forth. These will ultimately affect a company's profit picture, but jumping to conclusions at this stage could cost you more than a dissatisfied customer.

The second factor is anything that directly affects the bottom line of the business—profit. When we talk about continuous improvement, there is no savings too small. But if it is going to cost dollars to save pennies, the investment should not be made. The return-on-investment criterion is the most frustrating for the problem solver. After expending considerable time and effort to solve a problem we find out that our solution cost too much. Don't get frustrated; get busy. Throughout this entire book you have been asked to be creative; don't stop now. Take the solution back to the drawing board and take the frills off of it. It is normal on the first pass to have some "nice-to-haves" buried in the costs. Take the "fix" back down to bare bones and look at the costs and their impact. A simple way of doing this is to develop a cost sheet similar to the example shown here, but suited to your business.

Date: ____________

Return on Investment Documentation:

Describe the current situation: ______________________________
____
____

Describe the corrective action: ______________________________
____
____

What is the anticipated savings per piece ?..................... $ ________
What is the monthly volume ?.. x ________ **Pcs.**
Savings per month =

What are the costs to implement your idea:

New tools .... $ ____________
New machines .... $ ____________
Added maintenance cost ... $ ____________
Foundations .... $ ____________
Relocation expense .... $ ____________
Other .... $ ____________
Total cost $ ____________

Total cost ________ **/** ________ **Savings per month =** _______ **Months**

The number of months to repay the investment should be ____ or less.

Every company has a standard method for determining the return on investment of any project. To understand how acceptable your suggested solution is, determine how soon you will recover the costs of its implementation. Cost recovery is an important part of determining an effective solution to your problem.

RESOURCE REQUIREMENTS

Resources are the amounts of time, money, people, material, and so forth required to implement the solution and the extent to which they are available to the group. Resources relate directly to the costs of doing business. There must be good reasons for utilizing the resources of a business in the problem-resolution process, ones that relate to some of the other criteria previously discussed. Employee safety, customer satisfaction, improved quality, improved cost, and increased productivity are all good reasons to commit the resources of a business, because any of these will allow the business to better utilize its assets.

CONSENSUS

Consensus is the degree to which those affected by the changes are involved in implementing the solution. The greater their involvement the more acceptable the changes will be to them. This means getting people involved early on in the problem-solving process. If you do it right, the people who will commit the necessary resources have been in the problem-solving loop from the beginning. Consensus is not part of normal operating procedure in many businesses, which is one of the reasons for poor acceptance when a decision is made.

There may be other special criteria which should be added to this list. For example, the manager may have told you that there is no money available in the budget and that your solution must not cost anything. In this case you would add "no cost" to the list of criteria your solution must satisfy. Be aware of all special criteria prior to determining the final solution. Knowing all of the criteria ahead of time goes a long way toward avoiding the frustrations of finding out after-the-fact.

When you first review your list of possible solutions against this list of criteria, you may find that some are obviously inappropriate. Delete them from your list. Then reexamine the ones that remain. You must still make a final choice.

There are several tools that can assist you in making the final decision. These are designed specifically to make you process the information you have collected and reach a meaningful solution, not one that starts out with "I know in my heart that . . ."

THE SELECTION SPIDER

When you have reduced your list to a short list of the top three or four workable ideas, you may wish to evaluate and compare them to each other using the Selection Spider shown here. This tool works on the same principle as the Problem Spider in Step 1 of the problem-solving process (see Chapter 3). If you are working in a team or group, make sure you get a consensus opinion on the solution to be adopted.

Selection Spider Work Sheet ______________________________

Goal Statement: ______________________________

____

____

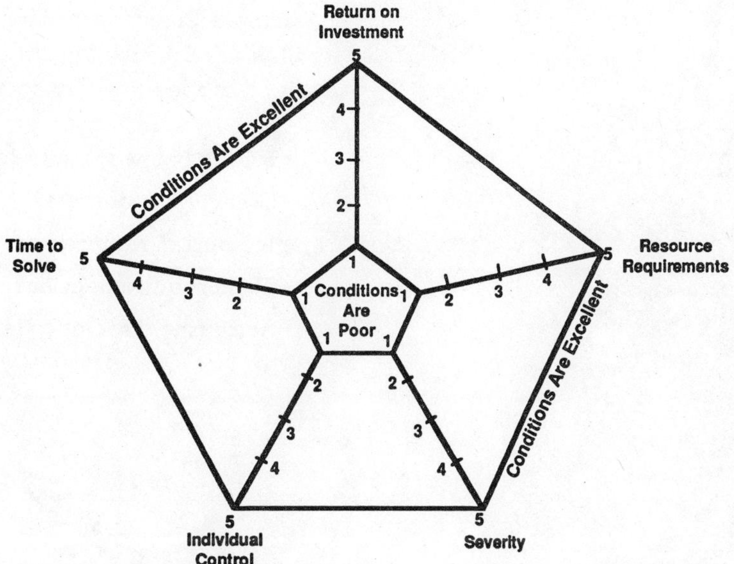

The Selection Spider

To use the Selection Spider to rate possible solutions you must follow each step carefully and be sure you clearly understand the definitions of the five points. Remember that you must fill out a separate evaluation for each possible solution to the problem.

When you have assigned ratings for each of the five points, add them up. The higher the total score, the greater the possibility that you or your group can work effectively on the problem.

Note that the scale is not the same for each item. The reason for this is that the greater the amount of control, seriousness, and return on investment, the better the chance of working on the problem. When it comes to resources and difficulty, these must be offset by the other categories. Be careful to get it right.

DEFINITIONS

Review briefly the points of the diagram; they are covered more fully at the beginning of this chapter and in Chapter 3 (see pages 44–46).

- Control
- Seriousness
- Time to Solve
- Return on Investment
- Resources

A sample Selection Spider is shown here. In our sample the total points are 14, making this a questionable solution. Why questionable? Let's look briefly at each category.

- ROI is below the mid-level.
- Control is moderate.
- Resources required are above average.
- Time requirement has been determined to be lengthy.
- Seriousness seems to be moderate.

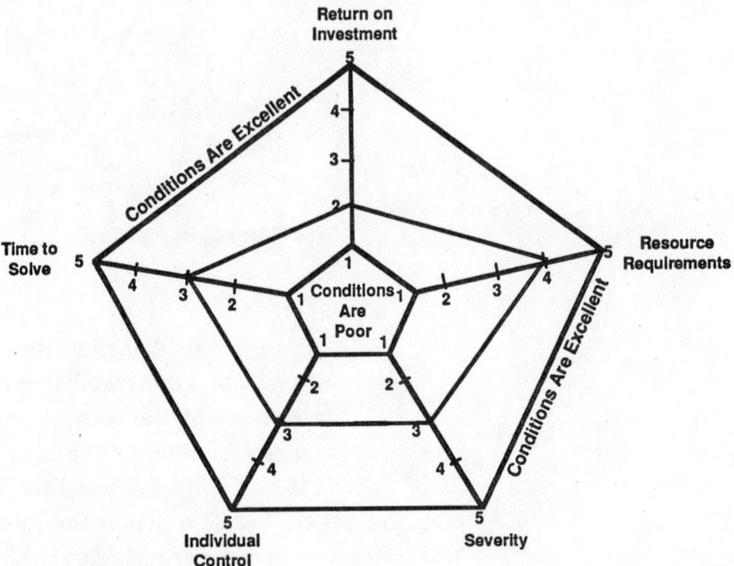

The key, again, is to rate all of the possible solutions in the same way. Once you have done that the raw scores will assist you in selecting the best one.

SELECTION FLOW DIAGRAM

- The selection flow diagram will identify solutions that fit the current criteria.
- The selection flow diagram will measure the solutions that best fit the criteria.

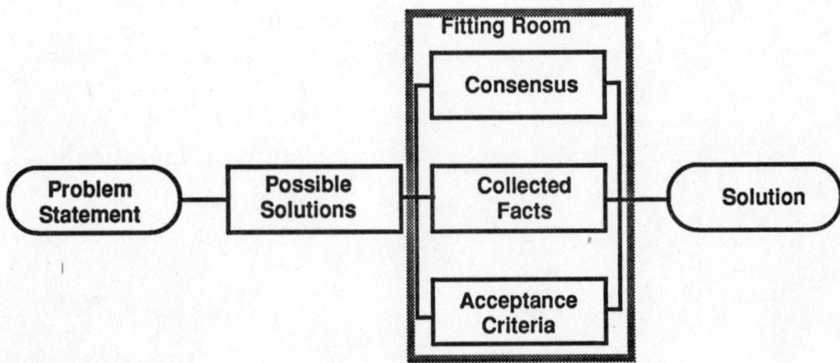

Selection Decision Process

This tool, the Selection Decision Process, is a flowchart designed to walk you through all the steps of the process required to make the final selection. The steps in using the selection flow diagram are as follows:

- Everything starts with the problem statement. Make sure that it still describes the existing condition.
- The next step is to review all of the possible solutions left after sorting through them, using any or all of the previously mentioned tools.

Entering the fitting room:

- In the fitting room you analyze the possible decisions, matching them against the data you have collected and the decision criteria, using consensus as the key to developing the final solution. When more than one of the possible solutions will "fix" the problem, consensus becomes a primary factor in the selection process. Group buy-in will assure the outcome. There are some other questions you should ask yourself or the group prior to making the final selection. They may seem redundant, but it is better to be safe than sorry.

FINAL REVIEW QUESTIONS

- If you implement this solution, what part of the problem will be solved and what part will not be?
- Could implementing this solution in fact cause problems elsewhere?
- Will this solution fix the problem permanently, or is it just a bandaid?
- Would this solution work better in combination with other possible solutions?

Again, asking these questions may result in your eliminating some of the possibilities on your list, or recombining them in a way that avoids any possible disadvantages. When you have completed your analysis you will have identified your preferred solution. Will you need approval to proceed before you move on to implementation? If so, you will need to present your findings. To assist you in this area I have included a simple outline for making a presentation.

PRESENTING YOUR FINDINGS

Find out what kind of approval you may need in order to proceed. Different types of solutions require different levels of approval. To get approval, you may be asked to make a presentation of your proposal. If so, follow these guidelines.

- *Introduction.* To get the attention of the group, the first step is to introduce yourself and explain why you are there and what you hope to accomplish in the time they have allotted to you. The explanation should be done in summary form (very little detail).

- *Problem Statement.* Provide the group with a clear understanding of the problem. Don't be afraid to say that once you began investigating the situation your view of the problem changed.
- *Need to Change.* Tell the group why it is important to change the current method of operation. Thoroughly explain the current situation and its pitfalls. Point out the waste involved, or the conditions that create waste, or other objectionable consequences. Provide graphics and pictures if possible.
- *Solution.* Give a clear explanation of your proposed solution. Again, provide graphics and pictures if possible. Also provide support information (i.e., cost data, etc.).
- *Benefits.* Describe in detail the benefits of adopting your proposal. This would include all factual data regarding costs, customer satisfaction, inventory turns, and increases in productivity. Benefits should outweigh costs if possible. Again, the challenge is to increase your company's competitive edge. Remember, pictures are worth a thousand words.
- *Summarize.* Provide the group with a brief summary. Restate the problem, the solution, and the benefits.

Remember,

- Allow time for questions.
- Be prompt in your presentation. Start and finish on time.
- Thank the group for their time.

GENERAL RULES

If it is a group proposal, let the individual doing the actual presentation write the material. Although the whole group should have a say on content, the presentor should do the actual graphics and text. This allows him or her to feel comfortable when making the presentation.

If more than one member of the group is to be present when the presentation is made, there should be an agreement that the presentor has the floor at all times, and that if the presentor needs help from the other members, he or she will ask.

Never pass out written material prior to the presentation; you will lose the group if you do. Most people will spend their time reading and fail to listen to the important details being presented.

Once approval is received, move on to implementation, Step 5 of the problem-solving process. The first thing you will do is plan the implementation.

Chapter 7

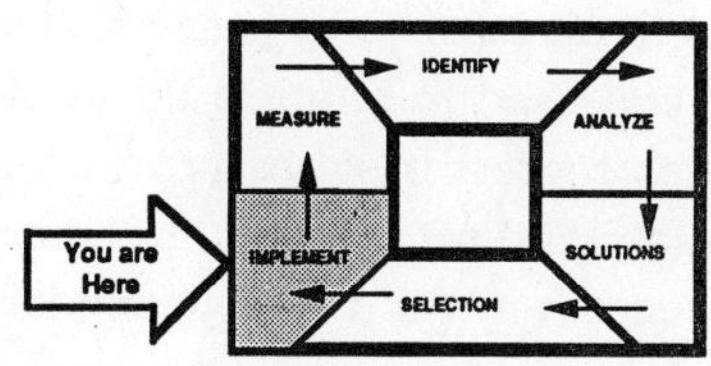

THE IMPLEMENTATION PROCESS

PLANNING THE IMPLEMENTATION

There are several planning techniques you can use to implement the solution you have selected. Some of these are flowcharts, Gantt charts, and pert charts. All require that you follow some basic steps. In this chapter I will discuss the Gantt chart and flowcharts. If you have a need for a pert or other type of planning chart, references are provided at the end of the book.

Good planning starts with these basic procedures:

- *Specify and clarify all tasks.* These include everything that must be done in order to implement the solution. Determine what must happen and write it down. This means everything!
- *Sequence the tasks.* Ask in what order they should be done. Some tasks depend on each other and so will have to precede or follow others. In performing this exercise you will learn about dependent and independent actions. The question is, When can the next action start?
- *Assess the resources and timing.* Ask who and what is required and to do what. As part of this step it is important that you determine how long it will take.
- *Establish a schedule.* Include targets and completion dates for each task. Remember that if your plan requires many different actions in sequence, a slip in the schedule in one part will affect all the other parts of the plan that depended on the item that was delayed. When you plan your timetable, be sure the people necessary to the plan's implementation will be present. Look at vacation schedules, meeting schedules, and other activity schedules to ensure that your plan is realistic.
- *Make sure everyone knows who is responsible for each task.* Be sure also that you have sufficient contact with the people who will be involved or affected by the solution as it is implemented. The communication of your plans—and later of the results—is an important part of implementing the solution effectively. Plan your checkpoints for communications like any other part of your plan.
- *Specify the results you expect and the times at which you will evaluate progress.* You must have standards of accomplishment

which will tell you whether your solution is actually solving the problem, and you must be able to measure your progress. Often, the same statistical measures you used to analyze the problem can also be used to demonstrate progress in solving it. As part of your implementation plan, understand what kind of information is required to determine the success or failure of your planned "fix." Once the criteria have been determined, don't compromise. Again, the most important thing you must deal with is the solution to the problem. Don't be afraid to say that you only solved half of it. This becomes a problem only if you fail to finish the job.

- *Finally, anticipate any obstacles.* It is better to plan ahead for things to go wrong and make contingency arrangements than to be surprised and embarrassed because you didn't think ahead. Your contingency plans can be written down as a series of "What if" statements in a secondary plan.

When you have worked out what needs to be in your plan, write it down on the plan form. You may also want to make a time chart to show what actions will be taking place simultaneously, how many will overlap, and when they will be completed relative to each other. Once you have done this you have an action plan to solve the problem.

EXERCISE Working with the problem you identified earlier, fill in the following:

Specify all of the tasks to be done in order to implement the "fix":

____

____

____

____

____

____

Place the tasks to be completed in the order that they must be done:

____

____

____

____

____

____

____

____

____

Using your resource chart, determine who is the natural owner of each of the tasks necessary to complete the implementation process:

For each task, contact the person assigned to it and determine the amount of time required for completion. Copy the sequence list in the first column of the chart, then complete the chart as the information becomes available.

Description of Task	Assigned to:	Time to Complete

THE FOLLOW-UP AND THE ANTICIPATED RESULTS

When getting your commitment on timing, there is only one basic rule that prevails: *make sure the person understands exactly what is expected.*

Periodically check with each person to make sure they are going to bring their part of the job in on time. It is better to know, and to be able to plan around shortfalls, than to find out at the last minute that the plan has fallen apart.

Two of the tools used in the planning process are the Gantt chart and flowcharts. Examples of these and how to use them are in the "tool box" that follows.

TOOLS TO HELP YOU PLAN

GANTT CHARTS

Gantt charts will identify:

- What must happen
- When it must happen
- Who must make it happen

Gantt charts will measure:

- Your current position in the project

A Gantt chart will assist you in organizing the tasks necessary to implement your solution. The Gantt chart puts in pictorial form the tasks, timing, resources, targets, and responsibilities required to complete the implementation process. Another advantage is that the interrelationship of the tasks is clear:

- An *independent task* does not rely on the completion of any other task. It can be started at any time. However, it may have one or more other tasks dependent on its completion.
- A *dependent task* depends on other tasks being completed prior to its being started.

In the sample Gantt chart illustrated here, which is typical in format, we determined that the steps necessary to implement the solution were to be as follows:

Order	*Action*	*Resp.*	*Ind./Dep.*	*Days to Complete*
1	Design new layout	B.C.	Dep.	5
2	Estimate costs	B.C.	Ind.	2.5
3	Get approvals	B.C.	Dep.	2
4	Order materials	B.C.	Dep.	4
5	Remove old equipment	J.D.	Ind.	7.5
6	Start new construction	J.D.	Dep.	9
7	Build required floats	P.M.	Ind.	10

Next, we developed the Gantt chart using these events and their timing. Our first step was to develop the scale in the timing area; this can be changed to suit any project. The scale we have chosen is weeks, with a total number of six being required to complete the project.

After laying out the chart, make your first entry. In this case it would be the design of the floor layout.

Step	What	Who	Timing in Weeks					
			1	2	3	4	5	6
1	New Floor Layout	B.C.						
2								
3								
4								
5								
6								
7								
8								
9								

Gantt Chart (A)

Using the information from our table, we can now go ahead and fill out the remainder of the chart. With all of the steps filled in, the chart would look like Gantt Chart (B).

Step	What	Who	Timing in weeks					
			1	2	3	4	5	6
1	New Floor Layout	B.C.						
2	Estimate Cost	B.C.						
3	Get Approvals	B.C.						
4	Order Materials	B.C.						
5	Remove Old Equip.	J.D.						
6	Start Construction	J.D.						
7	Build Floats	P.M.						
8	Start-up	All						
9								

Gantt Chart (B)

The Gantt chart shows the essentials of working a problem to completion. With this style chart we have the sequence of events, the task to be completed, the responsible party, and the estimated time for completion.

FLOWCHARTS USED FOR IMPLEMENTATION

Flowcharts will identify:

- Job sequence
- Activity interferences

Flowcharts will measure:

- Your current position in the project

Flowcharts are often used in project planning. Like the Gantt chart, what you must be aware of are the independencies and dependencies of some of the activities.

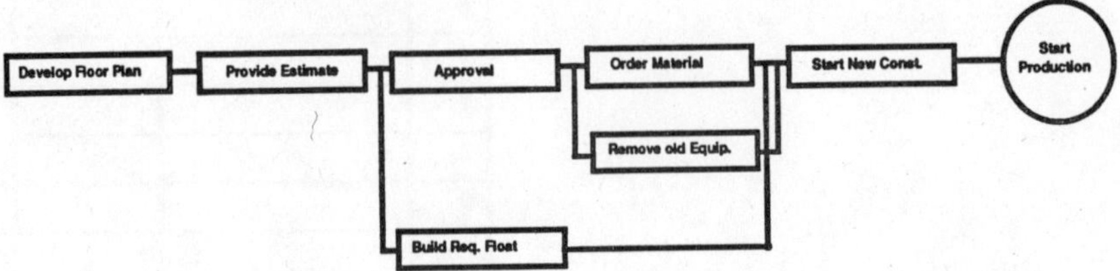

The flowchart offers us the opportunity to view the implementation plan and, if necessary, determine if alternative paths are required. In our example the same information was used to build the flowchart and the Gantt chart. As you can see, this example of a flowchart offers no event timing. Timing can be added to the flow diagram. The next step up from the flowchart is the pert network, or critical path diagram. Although volumes have been written about the pert networking, one of the simplest and most concise descriptions I have found can be located in a book called *100 Management Charts* by Soichiro Nagashima (see the list of references at the end of the book).

IMPLEMENTING THE PROCESS

This step involves actually doing what your plan said you would do and constantly checking to ensure that the actions are taking place according to the plan.

Here are some ideas for implementing the process:

- Make sure that the communication process keeps everyone informed about what is happening—the plan, the goal, and how effectively things are being done. Short daily meetings can help in keeping communications open.
- Take nothing for granted. CHECK, CHECK, CHECK.
- Be sure everyone knows what they have to do, and stay in close touch with those working on the project.
- Include everyone affected by the solution in the process.

- Divide the solution into easily manageable steps that can be monitored.

START EVALUATING IMMEDIATELY

Track and measure improvement using the same statistical methods you used to analyze the problem. Put the results on the chart for everyone to see.

Are the results what you expected? If so, *congratulations!* Make sure that everyone who contributed gets the recognition they deserve. Also, *share* the solution with others. It may apply in other areas.

If the results are not what you expected, then find out why not. You may have uncovered another problem—or, to put it another way, another opportunity.

HELPFUL HINTS FOR FUTURE PLANNING

After your plan has been implemented, it is time to make an overall evaluation of its success. There are two points to check:

- Did it go according to the plan?
- Have you in fact reached the goal?

Evaluate each separate part of the goal, using statistical methods and/or qualitative measurements of the effect (see Chapter 8). How much were costs reduced? How much was quality improved? If your evaluation shows that the results you expected are not occurring, there are several possible causes. Ask the following questions:

- Was the problem properly defined?
- Were the causes properly identified?
- Was the solution adequate?

It will be necessary to reenter the problem-solving process in order to identify the real problem and to develop a solution. If, on the other hand, the problem was successfully resolved, the next thing to do is to take steps to ensure that it does not reoccur. The methods for this are as follows:

- Standardize the new procedure or approach. This can be accomplished by using one of the following:
  - Written job instructions
  - Written quality instructions for quality checks
  - Routing changes
  - Written maintenance procedures
  - Boundary samples
- Establish control devices to ensure continued use of the new approach, and instruct others in the new procedures.
- Communicate what has been learned.

Chapter 8

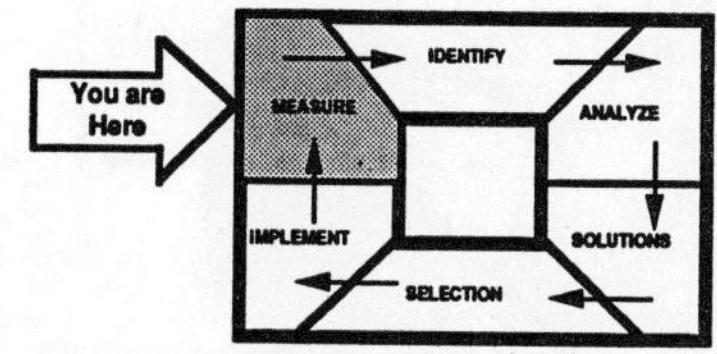

MEASUREMENTS THAT PREVENT REOCCURRENCE

It is in this last step of the problem-solving process that you must build into the manufacturing process the checks and balances necessary to ensure ongoing customer satisfaction. If you have always been involved in nonscientific methods of problem solving you are now probably congratulating yourself for "a job well done," ready to move on to the next problem, only to find out at some point in the future that you are faced with the same problem all over again.

Believing that you can stop once you have selected and implemented a solution is a way of thinking that you must now set aside. System checks must now be put into place. The term "permanent fix" means that you have not only solved the problem but have put into a place a measurement system to prevent reoccurrence.

The types of problems you already have, or will be working with, are those that involve correcting a specific situation (the unexpected problem) or making a known situation better (the anticipated problem). Both types are at the heart of the continuous improvement process. To ensure continuous improvement, the organization must move out of the "detection mode" and into the "prevention mode" of process or system management. Prevention is what will ensure customer satisfaction.

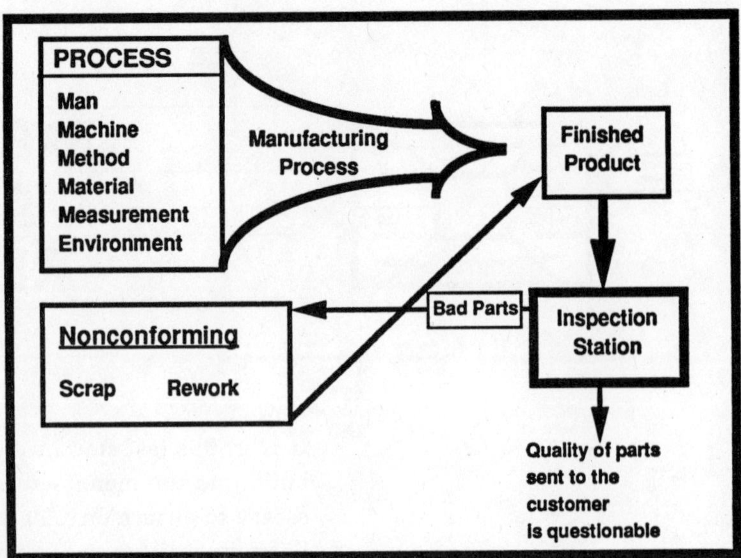

Detection Mode

DETECTION MODE OF OPERATION

The detection mode of system management, as illustrated here, is more concerned with quantity than quality, and each person in the system is left on his or her own to perform a specific part of the manufacturing operation.

In the first step of the detection mode of operation, the resources of the business are driven to produce a finished product, products that the business can sell in the marketplace. The people involved are normally told that it is their responsibility to produce and to set aside the obvious mistakes, and that the inspectors in the system will pass judgment on all of the other parts produced. In this method of operation, the inspector becomes the judge-and-jury of the part's quality, and the operator has no sense of having been responsible for producing a quality part. As the sorter, the inspector will find some parts that fail to meet the blueprint specifications. It is then his or her job to determine if that part should be reworked or scrapped. The parts to be scrapped are thrown out and those to be reworked are sent to the repair department. Once repaired, the parts are returned to the inspector who once again passes judgment on the parts.

There are some flaws in this style of operation. The first and most blatant is that no amount of after-the-fact inspection will make the *process* any better. In fact, this method almost ensures that defective material will find its way to the customer. This is because, and it can be proven statistically, 100% inspection will only find 85 percent of the defects. This means that the parts being sent to the customer contain defects not found by the inspector.

The second is that, unknowingly, you have set up a second department within the production system, the department now responsible for doing the rework and repairs. I am not saying that you should never do repairs, but I am saying that you should not have a portion of the work force dedicated to that purpose. The fact is that repairs add costs to the product and tie up equipment and manpower that could be utilized in making quality parts.

Also, in this mode of operation, controlling scrap and rework costs is extremely difficult. The reason for this is that when poor-quality parts are not detected as they pass from operation to operation, they begin to show themselves at or after final inspection. We have set up a situation where we must first sort the line for scrap or rework, and we run the risk of having dissatisfied customers due to the fact that we were unable to capture all of the poor-quality parts. Our ultimate task is to *prevent* the problem from reoccurring.

THE PREVENTION MODE

To ensure that the problem does not reoccur, we must put into place some procedure or system that guarantees that the problem will be controlled *at its point of origin*. Only by doing this can we ensure the quality of what is being produced. Graphically, a "prevent system" looks like the one illustrated here.

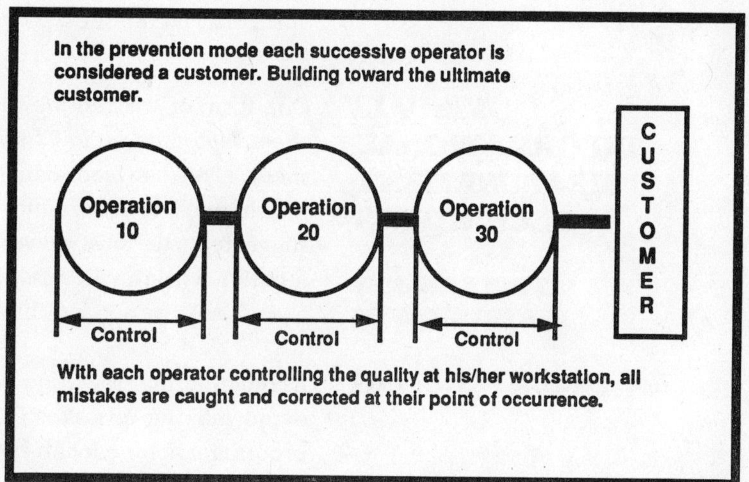

Prevention Mode

As you can see, the prevention mode of operation requires that each operator be responsible for all of the activities at his or her workstation. In this situation the operator is called the workstation manager and is recognized as being an intelligent and responsible individual, willing to account for his or her daily activities.

Control, as illustrated on the Prevention Mode chart, relates to overseeing the quality of the part, as well as other product-related responsibilities, for example, tool changes, quality checks, gage accuracy and machine repeatability. As part of his or her responsibility, the operator must understand some basic principles:

- What they do makes a difference.
- If it's not quality it doesn't go.
- Statistical methods must be used to monitor the process.
- All employees must have a common focus.
- No job is more important than any other.
- Everybody's ideas are important.

Once the decision is made to move from the detection mode to the prevention mode of factory floor operation, it is important to understand that it takes a great deal of time and a great deal of effort to make it happen. It is not something that happens overnight, and because of this it can be very frustrating to the operator, who may want to go back to the old way of doing things without really giving the prevention mode a chance.

As problems are corrected, take whatever measures are necessary to limit or stop them from reoccurring. Measurement techniques can be broken down into two types, visual/information techniques and statistical techniques.

VISUAL/ INFORMATIONAL MEASUREMENT TECHNIQUES

WRITTEN JOB INSTRUCTIONS

One form of written job instructions is the workstation design work sheet talked about in Chapter 4. Another form is the picture process sheet. The one common thread that runs through all written job instructions is clear and concise "how-to" instructions. Of those suggested, the most powerful is the workstation design used in conjunction with the picture process sheet. The first provides the "what-to-do" and the second the "how-to."

ERROR PROOFING

Error-proofing techniques are typically used to help employees avoid making mistakes. Simple mechanical methods, such as foolproofing machine locators so that parts cannot be loaded incorrectly, to more sophisticated electronic techniques, such as laser measurement to determine configuration of incoming parts, are all error-proofing techniques. No solution to a problem should be considered complete until error-proofing methods have been thoroughly investigated. Remember, the idea is to prevent problems from reoccurring.

BOUNDARY SAMPLES

Boundary samples, comparable to the go/no-go gages used to determine the relative size of a drilled hole, are used to determine the acceptable-quality levels of sheet metal or other parts where the discrepancies are observable. Sample parts showing the acceptable and unacceptable discrepancies are set aside and used as a reference when questions come up concerning the quality standards for that part. Actual parts should be used as boundary samples and kept in the work area where they are used.

Boundary samples are also used for statistical charts that use attribute data. These charts are shown later in this chapter.

STATISTICAL MEASUREMENT TECHNIQUES

Like problem solving, statistics is a science, a science that studies mathematical information. As a science it assists you in analyzing and then interpreting information into a usable form. It is based on the laws of probability, and uses random sampling to predict what outcomes will be. Used as a tool to improve the manufacturing process, statistics involves collecting relevant data and turning it into usable information. Statistics as a process-improvement tool has been around for some time, but not until more recent times has it been adopted by U.S. industry.

Why sampling? You can learn as much or more about your process by sampling than you can by 100% inspection. Sampling also has some other advantages:

- It is less time-consuming than 100% inspection.
- It is less expensive than 100% inspection.
- It may be more accurate than 100% inspection.
- It may be the only way to get the job done.

As an example of this last statement, think what the manufacture of flash cubes would entail if they 100% inspected the product. Now think about how many flash cubes you have seen fail. Statistics is a very powerful tool in dealing with the reduction of variation.

Rather than learn about the "how-to's" of statistics, let's talk about why we use statistical methods to observe our processes. Variation! Variation is the reason a machine or process generates scrap or rework. In the process of solving your problem you have been attempting to determine the following:

- How much variation your process or product has?
- How much variation will the process or product tolerate?
- How much does it change over time?
- What causes the change?
- How can the variation be reduced?

The first three represent how a problem is identified or selected as a problem. The last two represent the challenge of the problem-solving process itself. What you have been looking for while working through your problem is the amount by which the process varies. Variation has two causes, common and special. In the early stages of problem-solving a manufacturing process you will typically deal with the special, or assignable, causes of variation.

Special causes of variation represent a sudden shift from the norm, for example, unusual tool breakage or a sudden change in rework or repair. We have learned to live with certain common causes of variation. They may be product or process design problems that have caused us to make scrap or to rework. Today these areas must be viewed as opportunities for improvement.

In any problem-solving activity, the real challenge is to recognize the amount of variation the process generates initially and after the correction has been made. This is continuous improvement.

Statistical methods of measurement allow you to find out what has happened and what is likely to happen in your process or to your product. It is not my intention to teach statistics, only to give some definition and direction. I have selected several good textbooks for learning statistical techniques. These are listed at the end of the book.

First, let's identify some types of statistical tools that you can use to measure the outcome of your problem-solving activities. Histograms and $\bar{X}$ & R (median and range) charts use *variables data* that can be measured in quantitative terms. Inches, feet, millimeters, pounds, and foot pounds are all examples of variables data that can be accurately measured. $\bar{X}$ & R charts are the two most common types of charts used to manage variables data. Histograms were explained in Chapter 4. What I will do in this chapter is demonstrate a simple method of determining how successful the solution has been.

Other kinds of statistical tools use *attribute data* to determine the current condition of a process, for example, p charts, np charts, and C charts. Attribute data can be subjective: a person's senses may be determining the amount of variation in a process. The sense of feel is important when using a go/no-go gage; vision is important when looking for defects in a surface; and hearing is important if you are attempting to judge the output of radio speakers. We are all different, and so will not judge these outcomes identically. Moreover, don't let your judgment be influenced by what others say or do.

The simple truth is, none of us wants to be viewed as "different." If someone says, "That radio sounds good to me," then more than likely we will go along.

Let's talk about some of the terms used in statistics and what we hope to accomplish by using statistical methods. Let's start with one of the more misleading terms, "in control." To be "in control" does not necessarily mean that everything is all right. In fact, a process can be all wrong and still be in statistical control. "In control" means to be within statistically determined control limits. These calculated limits found on control charts have no relationship to blueprint specifications. Called the upper and lower control limits, they represent the mathematical limits that a process should be capable of running within. They are determined by the statistical sampling of a process without tampering with the process itself. You take the sample averages and by placing them in the correct formulas determine the control limits of the process. If all of the points are inside the upper and lower control limits, and no special conditions exist, the process is said to be "in control." A process can be in control statistically and still be making all bad parts. We discuss statistical control again later on in the chapter.

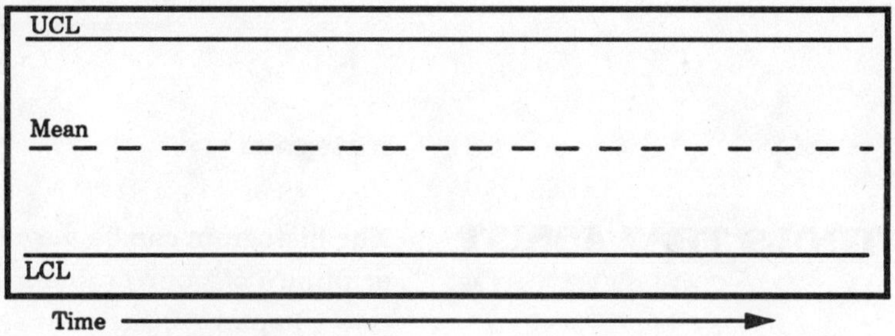

UCL

Mean

LCL

Time →

Process Control Chart

GAGE AND MACHINE CAPABILITY

Gage and machine capability studies should be performed as part of your quality control plan. There is no real need to wait until you are in a problem-solving situation to perform gage and machine capability studies. Gage capability studies should be performed prior to recording any variables data readings. This will ensure the accuracy of the information collected.

The machine capability study ensures the repeatability of the process itself. For this reason any negative outcomes on the machine capability study should be corrected prior to moving forward with any additional data collection. There are several good sources for the "how-to's" of machine and gage capability. All I can suggest that you adopt a companywide method of control and stick to it. Be sure all involved parties know what must be done to prevent problems from reoccurring.

Some of the tools that will allow us to measure the results of our problem-solving efforts are discussed on the following pages. Again, it is not my intention to provide a complete "how-to" on industrial statistics, but to introduce you to some of the terminology and visual examples of what the user should be looking for. All of these samples should be viewed as "thought-starters" only.

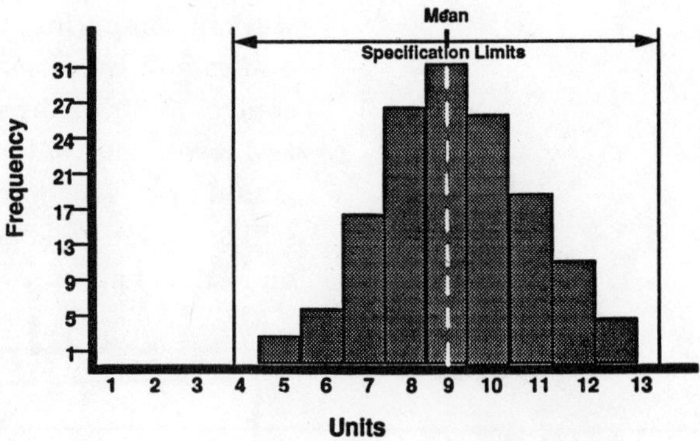

Histogram

TOOLS THAT ASSIST IN CONTROL

HISTOGRAMS

The histogram can be very helpful to you in determining the success or failure of your problem-solving activities. Once data is collected (see Chapter 4), the next step in the process is to place, on the histogram, the specifications limits, and the calculated mean of the process. You can now visualize how the process is running. Remember, a histogram is only a picture of a process taken at one moment in time, and should not be used to predict how the process will run over time. To evaluate a process over time you must use process control charts.

PROCESS CONTROL CHARTS

Statistical process control charts are the best way of controlling your manufacturing processes, although, as I said earlier, the word "control" can be misleading. The $\bar{X}$ & R—or median and range—type of control chart is used when variables measurements can be taken. Variables data are any kind of data that can be specifically measured. Gage readings, pressure readings, and temperature are a few examples of variables data.

$\bar{X}$ & R charts

$\bar{X}$ & R charts will identify:

- Process changes
- Variation over time
- Process capability
- Processes that are out of control

$\bar{X}$ & R charts will measure:

- Process range
- Process average
- Process capability

The $\bar{X}$ & R chart allows us to observe our process continuously over long periods of time. When process improvements are made, we can visually recognize any increase or reduction in the amount of variation in the process. A sample of a blank $\bar{X}$ & R chart is illustrated here.

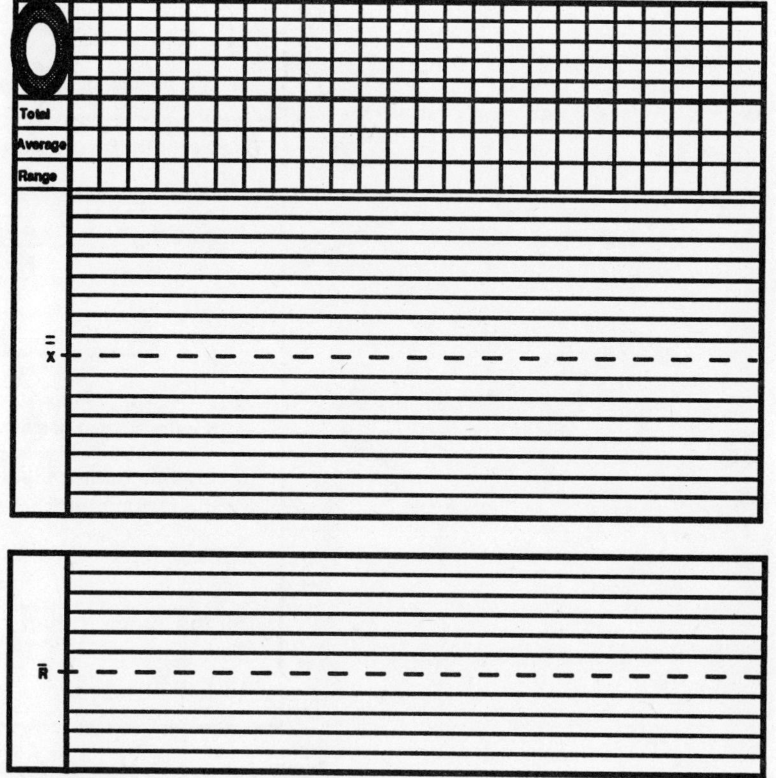

$\bar{X}$ & R Chart

Following are a variables data chart and the formulas necessary to calculate the data, both of which you will need to complete the $\bar{X}$ & R chart. As pointed out earlier, there are several excellent books on statistics. Please refer to any of the books listed in the reference section for the "how-to's" of this subject.

Formulas for Variables Data

The formulas used to calculate the average ($\bar{X}$) and range (R) of each of the subgroups are

$$\bar{X} = \frac{X_1 + X_2 + \ldots X_n}{n}$$

$$R = X_{max} \; X_{min}$$

n = the number of samples

To calculate the grand average and range:

$$\bar{X} = \frac{\bar{X}_1 + \bar{X}_2 + \ldots \bar{X}_N}{N}$$

$$\bar{R} = \frac{R_1 + R_2 + \ldots R_N}{N}$$

N = the number of subgroups

To calculate control limits:

for the range chart:

$$UCL_R = D_4\bar{R} \qquad LCL_R = D_3\bar{R}$$

for the average chart:

$$UCL = \bar{\bar{X}} + A\bar{R}_2 \qquad LCL = \bar{\bar{X}} - A\bar{R}_2$$

Formulas for Variables Data

Number of observation in subgroup (n)	$\bar{X}$	R	
	A_2	D_3	D_4
3	1.02	0	2.57
4	.73	0	2.28
5	.58	0	2.11
6	.48	0	2.00
7	.42	.08	1.92
8	.37	.14	1.86
9	.34	.18	1.82
10	.31	.22	1.78

Variables Data Chart

Once you have determined what the control limits are to be, there are some simple methods of determining if a process is "in control." A process is considered to be "in control" if all of the samples fall randomly within the upper and lower control limits on both the median ($\bar{X}$) and range (R) charts. The chart here shows a process that is "in control."

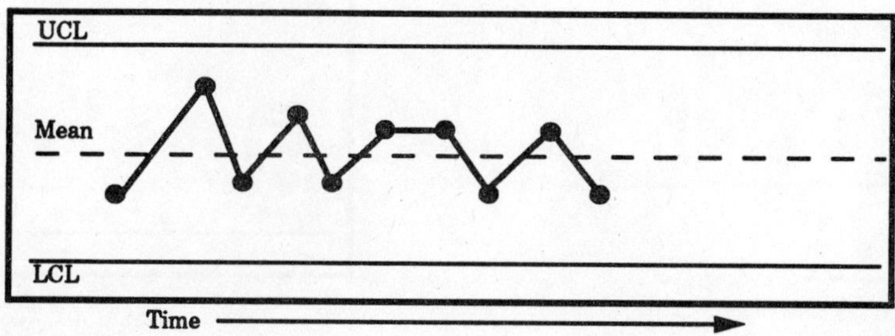

In Control

To determine if a process is out of control, there are some very simple rules. Let's look at a sample control chart with standard deviations. This could be either the median or the range portion of the chart $\bar{X}$ & R. There are three areas on either side of the mean. In statistical terms, each area represents one standard deviation. To be "in control," all of the process sample will fall within those areas in a random pattern.

Your process is considered to be out of control when the patterns become nonrandom. I would also like to point out that not all out-of-control conditions are bad. But, when a bad out-of-control condition does arise, it is essential that you find out what caused it.

UCL
Area 3
Area 2
Mean
Area 1
Area 1
Area 2
Area 3
LCL
Time

Control Chart with Standard Deviations

To tell if a process is out of control, some of the conditions to look for are as follows:

- Hugging—points stay close to the mean or either of the control limits.

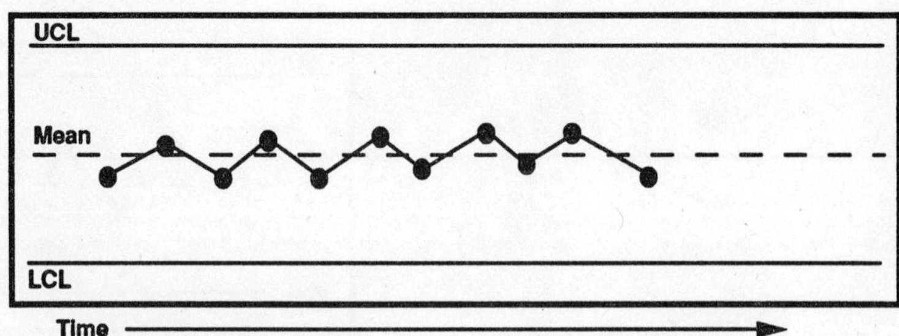

Out of Control—Hugging

Again, if you are hugging the mean, this indicates a favorable change in the process, but you must find out what caused it. If, however, you were hugging either the upper or lower limit on your median ($\bar{X}$) chart or the upper limit on the range (R) chart, indications are that you have a real problem.

- Runs—five or more consecutive points on either side of the process mean.

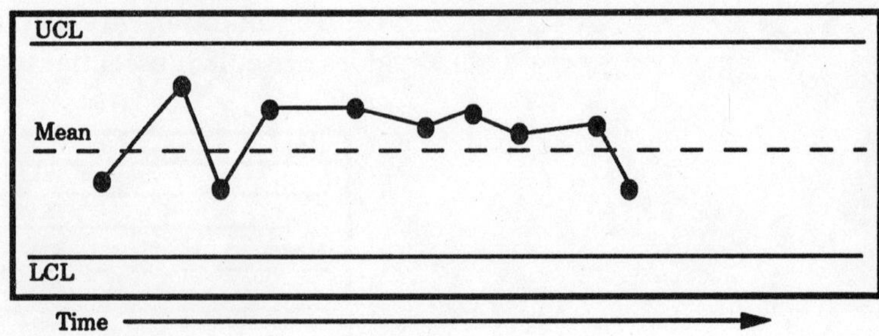

Out of Control—Runs

- Trends—seven or more points rise or fall.

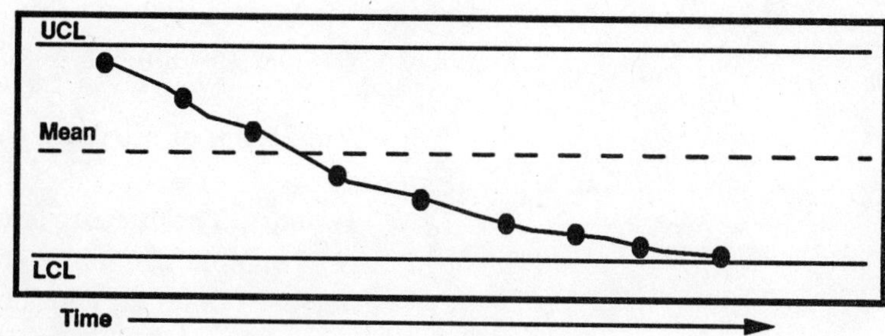

Out of Control—Trends

- Periodicity—points show the same pattern over equal time intervals.

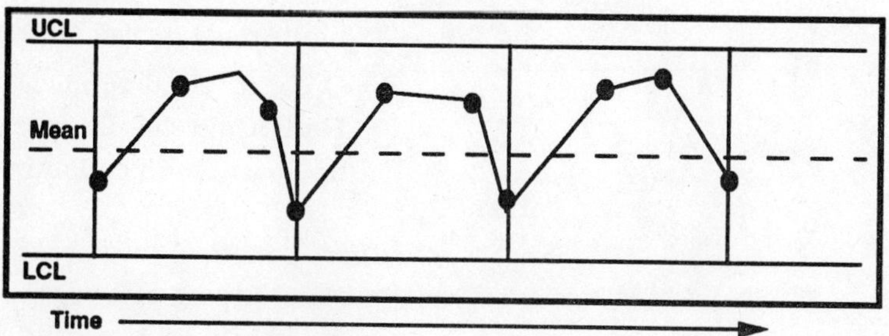

Out of Control—Periodicity

ATTRIBUTE CHARTS

Attribute charts will identify:

- Process changes
- Variation over time
- Process capability
- Processes that are out of control

Attribute charts will measure:

- Process range
- Process average
- Process capability

Attribute charts are another form of statistical process control charts. They are best used to control your manufacturing processes when there are no variables measurements available. Attribute data are any kind of data that must be measured in observable terms. Go/no-go gage types and defects/foot are types of attribute data.

The attribute chart, like the variables chart, allows us to monitor our process over long periods of time. When process improvements are made, this type of control chart allows us to observe the results by visually recognizing any increase or reduction in process variation.

Some types of attribute charts are as follows:

- p chart. The p chart is used to measure the percent defective. The sample size may vary, but you must calculate control limits for each point on your chart (every point).
- np chart. The np chart is used to measure the number of defects in each sampling. The sample size must be constant, but unlike the p chart you need only calculate one set of control limits.
- U chart. Used to measure the number of defects per unit. The sample size for a U chart is one or more, and what you are looking for is the number of defects found on those units. Control limits must be calculated on each sample.
- C chart. Used to measure the number of defects in a sample. Here again the size of the sample must be constant, but, like the np chart, you need only calculate one set of control limits.

Where practical, use control charts to measure the results of your problem-solving efforts. One of the more common questions about control charts is, How often do I take samples? The answer that I normally give is, As often as is practical, until you determine that the process is in control and capable. At that point you can start to back off on your sampling. I don't mean to go from seven or eight times per shift to once a day overnight, but to let the process do the talking. It will tell you that it is time to move from constant sampling to an audit mode.

You have just completed the six steps in the problem-solving process. The thing you must remember is to document what you are doing. This will keep you focused. It will also provide you with an audit trail to return to if the problem should reappear. In addition, you will have a history file for comparison purposes, allowing you to determine the contribution that was made by you or your group.

REFERENCES

H. C. Charbonneau & G. L. Webster
Industrial Quality Control
Prentice-Hall
Englewood Cliffs, N.J., 1978

DataMyte Corporation
DataMyte Handbook, 4th ed.
Minnetonta, Minn.

Laird Dugan
Approaches to Training and Development
Addison-Wesley
Reading, Mass., 1985

Ford Motor Company
Continuing Process Control & Process Capability Improvement
Dearborn, Mich., 1985

W. Gellert et al.
VNR Concise Encyclopedia of Mathematics
Van Nostrand Reinhold
New York, N.Y., 1977

Paul Hersey & Kenneth Blanchard
Management of Organizational Behavior, 5th ed.
Prentice-Hall
Englewood Cliffs, N.J., 1988

Kaoru Ishikawa
Guide to Quality Control
Asian Productivity Organization
Tokyo, Japan

Kaoru Ishikawa
What Is Total Quality Control?
Prentice-Hall
Englewood Cliffs, N.J., 1985

Japan Management Association
The Cannon Production System
Productivity Press
Stamford, Conn.–Cambridge, Mass., 1987

J. M. Juran & Frank M. Gryna, Jr.
Quality Planning and Analysis
McGraw-Hill
New York, N.Y., 1980

Robert F. Mager
Developing an Attitude Toward Learning
David S. Lake Publishers
Belmont, Calif., 1984

Robert F. Mager
Preparing Instruction Objectives
David S. Lake Publishers
Belmont, Calif., 1984

Richard E. Mayer
Thinking, Problem Solving, Cognition
W. H. Freeman
New York, N.Y., 1983

William Mendenhall
Introduction to Probability and Statistics
PWS Publishers
Boston, Mass., 1987

Soichiro Nagashima
100 Management Charts
Asian Productivity Organization
Tokyo, Japan, 1987

J. William Pfeiffer & Arlette C. Ballew
Presentation and Evaluation Skills
University Associates
San Diego, Calif., 1988

Barry L. Reece & Rhonda Brandt
Effective Human Relations in Organizations
Houghton Mifflin
Boston, Mass., 1987